lonely planet
food

THE WORLD'S BEST

BOWL
FOOD

WHERE TO FIND IT
& HOW TO MAKE IT

CONTENTS

FOREWORD

BY JANINE EBERLE

So, what is bowl food? In a sense it's the latest fad: paleo-macro-bio lunches served on the blond-wood tables of Edison-bulb-bedecked cafes. Dishes that launched a million #powerbowl Instagram posts and a fleet of food trucks.

But fads explode because they touch a deeper truth. As we put together this book exploring bowl foods around the world, it became clear that food just doesn't fall into bowls by accident. The things we eat from them have some common characteristics, from Iceland to Burma, Ghana to Peru. Whether it's a fiery chilli con carne, a long-simmered Welsh stew or a spicy mound of Moroccan couscous, these are meals that speak the international language of comfort.

They're the foods that go to the heart of a cuisine, and recall home, or childhood, or tradition. They're among the world's most beloved dishes – macaroni and cheese, Vietnamese pho, Japanese rāmen. These bowls have transcended their local roots and become transcontinental comfort meals.

You'll find some recurring themes. What cuisine doesn't have a cure-all chicken soup? From Jewish chicken and matzo ball to Greek avgolemono to Korean samgyetang, the art of concocting medicine from fowl meat has long been a global pursuit. There's the ancient art of nose-to-tail eating, slow-cooking to make the best of less desirable cuts of meat, from France's boeuf bourguignon to South African bredie. Crafty ways to concoct deliciousness from yesterday's leftovers, like Levantine fattoush built around stale pitta bread, to Indonesia's nasi goreng, using up rice from the night before. The resourcefulness of peasant home cooks has brought us some of our most loved meals.

It's not surprising that in a modern world where eating healthily has, in many cases, replaced the need for eating thriftily, we've returned to the bowl as a symbol for all that makes us feel good about food. The triumph of casual eating over formal dining and our predilection for dining while sitting on the sofa watching TV also make the bowl a natural choice of vessel.

And then there's what Oxford University's expert in the psychology of taste Charles Spence calls the 'multisensory' nature of eating – if you hold the bowl while eating from it, its weight may lead you to feel more satisfied with the meal. Foodie thought leaders have stepped up to the plate – or rather, bowl – with Gwyneth Paltrow and Nigella Lawson among the leading exponents of bowl-based eating; Nigella defines it as 'simply shorthand for food that is simultaneously soothing, bolstering, undemanding and sustaining.'

And with this book of the world's ultimate bowls, we have to agree. Whether old-school meat-and-veg stew or fashion-forward grain salad, these bowls are feel-good food at its best. All hail the bowl.

BREAKFAST
BOWLS

They say it's the most important meal for good reason – waking up to a bowl of something nourishing sets you up for the day. Whether it's an oh-so-traditional bowl of porridge or something a little different like a Chinese *congee* or Quebec's favourite *fèves au lard*, there's nothing like a full belly to help you seize the day.

 Easy 🥣 🥣 Medium 🥣 🥣 🥣 Hard

ORIGINS

Chia is harvested from *Salvia hispanica*, a herb related to mint. Once as much a staple food as maize, it makes its first recorded appearance in the mid-1500s in the *Codex Mendoza*. This illustrated Aztec manuscript is written in Nahuatl language, in which *chian* means oily – a good indication of the seeds' high levels of omega 3. Reversing the colonial trend, in the late 20th century chia made a lasting incursion out of its central American heartland into kitchens and cafes around the world.

SERVES 2

CENTRAL AND SOUTH AMERICA

CHIA PUDDING

Delicious, nutritious chia seed has taken a long journey, from its ancient rural origins in the Americas to the menus of hip cafes and health-conscious kitchens across the world.

YOU'LL NEED

2 cups natural or flavoured yoghurt
½ cup chia seeds
2 tbs flaked almonds
honey, maple syrup or cream, to serve

VARIATIONS

For a thicker pudding, add more chia seeds
For choc-chia pudding, use good-quality cocoa made with hot milk instead of yoghurt
For vegan pudding, use coconut or soy yoghurt mixed with nut milk
For a more tangy pudding, use stewed fruit instead of yogurt

METHOD

1 In a large bowl, combine the yoghurt and chia seeds. Mix well using a whisk or fork.

2 Transfer to serving bowl, cover, and put in the fridge for 4 hours or overnight.

3 Heat a frying pan and dry-fry flaked almond until they turn light brown. Allow to cool, then put in an airtight container until ready to use.

4 Sprinkle flaked almond on to chia pudding just before serving.

5 Serve in bowls drizzled with honey, maple syrup or cream to taste.

TASTING NOTES

Happily, the contemporary trend for chia is due to more than its history and nutritional value. Chia seeds have a delicate, nutty flavour and their capacity to absorb liquid creates a slightly gelatinous smoothness and texture in milkshakes and desserts, making a delicious, filling, often sweetish and decidedly moreish bowl of comfort. In health-food delis, chia might appear alongside goji berries to thicken layers of stewed fruit or chocolate pudding, or give an extra kick to fresh juices. At home, throw a handful of raw seeds into homemade bread or muesli for an additional burst of flavour, texture and goodness, or add to quality yoghurt for a simple, stunning dessert or breakfast treat. ● *by Virginia Jealous*

YOU'LL NEED

1 cup medium grain rice
8 cups light chicken stock
salt
soy sauce
thinly sliced spring onions
  (scallions), green parts only
finely chopped fresh ginger
sesame oil
shredded chicken or soft-
  boiled egg, quartered
  (optional)

ORIGINS

A version of the dish known
in southern China as *zhou* is
found all over Asia, prepared
with millet, barley, cornmeal,
sorghum or mung beans. The
earliest reference to *congee*
dates it to the Han dynasty,
around AD 220, but some claim
that its origins go back to the
Zhou dynasty, around 1000 BC.
It evidently originated as a way
of stretching a meal in harsh
times, but it's also mentioned
in accounts of the meals
of emperors.

SERVES 2–3

CHINA

CONGEE

Asia's favourite comfort food, *congee* (or *okayu* in Japan, *juk* in
Korea, *chok* in Thailand – just to name a few) is traditionally eaten
for breakfast, but it's a bowl of restorative goodness at any time.

METHOD

1 Wash the rice well.

2 Put the rice in a pot with the chicken stock
and bring to boil. Stir the rice, scraping the
bottom of the pan to prevent sticking, then
lower the heat and half-cover the pot.

3 Simmer gently for 1½–2 hours, stirring
occasionally to prevent the rice from sticking,
until the grains have burst open and the
congee is thick.

4 Towards the end of the cooking time, when
the rice is almost at the desired consistency,
season lightly with salt to taste.

5 Serve in deep bowls with a sprinkling of soy
sauce, spring onion and ginger and a few drops
of sesame oil to taste. Top with shredded
chicken or egg, if using.

TASTING NOTES

Basic *congee* is as no-frills as a dish can be: rice cooked in plenty of water (or stock) for
so long that it disintegrates. That makes it a blank canvas on which personal tastes can be
freely expressed. First, consistency: thin like gruel, or thick like oatmeal? (Controlling the
consistency is simple: cook 1 cup of rice in 8 cups of water for a thick *congee*, 13 cups for
a watery one.) Next, choose your accompaniments: shredded pork and preserved egg, duck
and shiitake mushrooms, chicken gizzards. Eight-treasure *congee*, a luxurious dessert to
celebrate harvest, is made with dried dates, peanuts, lotus seeds, pine nuts and raisins.
As an elegant minimum, serve it straight up, steaming from the pot, with soy sauce and
sesame oil, thinly sliced spring onions and fresh ginger on the side. ● *by Janine Eberle*

ORIGINS

While beans were a staple food for many of Canada's aboriginal peoples, settlers migrating north from New England may have brought the method of baking them in a ceramic pot to Quebec, where these cooked-till-they're-creamy legumes sustained generations of pioneers and *voyageurs* (fur traders). The *lard* in *fèves au lard* is the Quebecois term for salt pork. Contemporary cooks can substitute more readily available bacon, or omit the meat entirely for a vegetarian version.

YOU'LL NEED

1 cup navy/haricot beans or other small dried white beans

1 small onion, peeled

1 tomato

3–4 slices bacon, thick-cut if possible

¼ cup maple syrup

2 tsp Dijon mustard

½ tsp salt

¼ tsp ground black pepper

QUEBEC, CANADA

FÈVES AU LARD

SERVES 2

In Quebec, *fèves au lard* – slow-cooked beans, rich with salt pork
and sweetened with maple syrup – are traditional breakfast fare,
fuel for adventures from canoeing to skiing to urban brunching.

METHOD

1 To soften beans, place them in a large bowl
well covered with water and let sit 8 hours or
overnight. Alternatively, 'quick soak' the beans
by covering them with water in a medium pot,
bringing to the boil, covering the pot, turning off
the heat, and letting them sit for about an hour.

2 Preheat the oven to 140°C (275°F).

3 Drain the beans and put them in a large
casserole or baking dish with a lid.

4 Coarsely chop the onion and tomato and
add to the beans.

5 Dice the bacon crosswise and add to
the beans and vegetables.

6 Add maple syrup, mustard, salt, pepper
and 2 cups water and stir to combine.

7 Cover baking dish, place in the oven, and
bake, stirring about once an hour. Add water if
necessary to ensure beans are always covered,
or they'll become tough. Bake until beans are
tender, about 6–7 hours.

8 If the dish seems very soupy but the beans
themselves are soft, remove the lid for the
last 30 minutes of cooking.

9 To serve the beans for breakfast, ideally
make them 1–3 days in advance; refrigerate
cooked beans and reheat them thoroughly
when ready to serve.

TASTING NOTES

Ask a Quebecois where to find the best *fèves au lard*, and many will respond 'chez ma
grand-mère'. But if you don't have a bean-baking grandmother, head for the home-style
diners across the province known as 'bineries'. In Montreal, La Binerie Mont-Royal serves
fèves for breakfast with everything from eggs to steak; a favourite morning option is a crock
of beans paired with toast and coffee. Another popular time to eat *fèves au lard* is during
the spring maple sugaring season, when rural sugar shacks such as Sucrerie de la Montagne
west of Montreal or Le Relais des Pins on Île d'Orléans pile their long wooden tables with
tourtières (meat pies), pancakes, sausages, and bowls of baked beans, sweetened, of
course, with maple syrup. ● *by Carolyn Heller*

VARIATIONS

Mix and match different fruit and spice combinations: almond meal, fresh grated or chopped crystallised ginger, cardamom pods or nutmeg. For vegan frumenty, substitute almond milk and maple syrup For savoury frumenty, use meat or chicken stock in place of water and serve alongside a hearty casserole.

ORIGINS

Frumenty gets its name from *frumentum*, the Latin word for grain. A traditional European winter food, it found its way to England in the Middle Ages. Frumenty became a staple food, and sweet and savoury versions developed locally according to season and occasion. During banquets, frumenty was served with venison; during meat-free Lent, only eggs were added for extra protein. It also plays a fateful role in Thomas Hardy's novel *The Mayor of Casterbridge*.

SERVES 4

ENGLAND

FRUMENTY

As an ancient traditional feast-dish of hot, spiced grains, frumenty appears in medieval cookbooks and early literature. As a contemporary home-cooked, cold-weather comfort food, it's hard to beat for breakfast.

YOU'LL NEED

1 cup pearl barley
2 tbs currants
3 cloves
2.5cm (1in) stick of cinnamon
3 cups water
1 cup milk
3 tbs honey, plus extra to serve
2 egg yolks (optional)
pouring cream, to serve

METHOD

1 Rinse the barley in a sieve under running water.

2 Transfer to saucepan and add cloves, cinnamon and currants.

3 Cover with cold water and bring to the boil. Simmer for 1–2 hours, adding more water if needed, until grains have absorbed all the water and are split, soft and sticky.

4 Whisk together the milk, honey and egg yolks. Add to the barley mixture and heat through.

5 Serve with cream and extra honey to taste.

NOTE *Frumenty also works well in a slow cooker or in a very low oven. Mix barley, spices and dried fruit and leave to cook for 4–6 hours. Stir in milk, honey and egg yolks about 30 mins before eating.*

TASTING NOTES

Imagine a cold, dark, don't-want-to-get-out-of-bed morning in mid-winter. Wafting through the bedroom door is the scent of the spiced hot frumenty that's been slow-cooking overnight. It's a perfect wake-up call. Morning tastebuds tingle with the smooth texture of individual cooked grains, the gentle zing of cooked ginger, the perfume of cardamom, the sweet energy of honey. A dollop of cream can best be described as the icing on the cake. Or imagine the other end of a winter day, perhaps getting home in the cold dark. Opening the front door, the smell of savoury frumenty welcomes with a hint of onion and cloves; a perfect way to wind down and warm up. ● *by Virginia Jealous*

ORIGINS

Egyptians have enjoyed broad (fava) beans since the time of the Pharaohs. At the end of each day, cooks placed tureens of beans upon the embers of smouldering fires at bath houses to slowly cook overnight into a flavourful stew. Egyptians so revered these beans that they also offered them to the gods. The recipe was exported across the Middle East and Africa. Today, *ful medames* is considered a national dish of Egypt.

YOU'LL NEED

260g (9oz) dried broad
  (fava) beans
5 garlic cloves
½ cup olive oil
juice of 1 lemon
¼ tsp cumin
½ tsp coriander powder
1 cup water
4 eggs
4 pita
tahini and extra olive oil,
  to serve (optional)
4 parsley sprigs, to garnish

TASTING NOTES

Even in frenetic Cairo, not everything happens in a hurry. And there's certainly no rushing a good *ful medames*. Before the city's chorus of car horns reaches a climax, when the early-morning fog is still draped over skyscrapers and minarets, Cairenes drift towards street vendors for a plateful. So follow the crowds (and your nose) when you choose a spot for breakfast. Liberal drizzlings of olive oil add to the rich, smoky flavour of the *ful*, which is best eaten by hand. Scoop it up with rounds of freshly baked bread, and cleanse your palate with pickled vegetables. '*Laziza*' (delicious) might be difficult to say with a mouthful of bread and *ful*, but your appreciative murmurs are sure to breach the language barrier. ● *by Anita Isalska*

EGYPT

FUL MEDAMES

SERVES 4

From street corners to five-star restaurants, Egyptians breakfast on a dish that has barely changed since 2000 BC: slow-cooked spiced broad beans loaded on to stone-baked flatbread.

METHOD

1 Soak the dried beans in a large bowl of cold water, ideally for about 12 hours.

2 Once the beans are plumped up with water, peel and crush the garlic cloves.

3 Heat the olive oil in a large frying pan.

4 Add the garlic, drained beans, lemon juice, cumin and coriander to the olive oil.

5 Stir the mixture over a low heat for 5 minutes, until the ingredients are well mixed and heated through.

6 Pour the contents of the pan into a slow-cooker (or see tip).

7 Add the water and leave the cooker on a low heat for about 12 hours (ideally overnight, so you can enjoy your *ful* in the morning). Stir the mixture occasionally.

8 In the morning, hard-boil the eggs in a pan of boiling water for 8 minutes.

9 Remove the eggs from the pan with a slotted spoon and place them straight into a bowl of cool water.

10 Allow the eggs to cool slightly, then peel off the shells.

11 Slice the hard-boiled eggs into quarters.

12 Toast the pita under a grill for 1 minute on each side.

13 Place one pita on each of four plates.

14 Place a ladleful of the slow-cooked beans next to each pita.

15 Drizzle the remaining olive oil on each serving of *ful*.

16 Top each portion with a small sprig of parsley and four egg quarters.

TIP *Using a slow-cooker is the best way to replicate the ancient method of making* ful medames, *and it ensures infusion of the spices. However, if you're short on time, or don't have a slow-cooker, boil the soaked beans for 1 hour before draining and mashing in the spices.*

ORIGINS

A type of muesli was first devised in the 1900s for its health benefits by Swiss doctor Maximilian Bircher-Benner, after which the Bircher muesli dish is named. Bircher muesli is a 'wet' combination of oats and water, with chopped apples, nuts, lemon juice and cream, topped with honey. Modern recipes sometimes call for healthier yoghurt in place of the cream. In later years, muesli took on various drier guises. Today, it's a permanent breakfast fixture.

EUROPE (ESPECIALLY SWITZERLAND
AND GERMANY), USA, AUSTRALIA AND UK

MUESLI

MAKES
8 CUPS

**Toasted or raw; three ingredients or 20; mushy or dry –
infinitely adaptable, muesli is simply one of the best choices
for breakfast or brunch and is packed with nutrition to boot.**

YOU'LL NEED

3 cups rolled oats
1 cup quinoa flakes
½ cup almonds, chopped
½ cup pumpkin seeds (or
   hemp seeds)
½ cup walnuts, chopped
1 cup sultanas (golden raisins)
½ cup dried apricots, roughly
   chopped
½ cup dried coconut flakes
   (unsweetened)
½ cup sunflower seeds
½ cup goji berries or dried
   cranberries
1 tbs ground cinnamon
dash of nutmeg
milk or yoghurt, to serve
fresh or stewed fruits, to serve

METHOD

1 Place the oats in a large bowl.

2 Add the remaining ingredients, apart from the yoghurt
and fruit.

3 Mix everything thoroughly using your hands or a large spoon.

4 Store the mixture in an airtight container in a cupboard (not
in the refrigerator).

5 When you are ready to eat it, put a portion in a bowl and
serve with milk or yoghurt and top with fresh or stewed fruits.

TIP *The best thing about muesli? As well as being tantalising,
nutritious, and easy to make and serve, all experimentation is
good experimentation. Bircher muesli aside, there's no 'correct'
muesli recipe. This means you can try any combination of seeds
and nuts – and perfect it to meet your own needs. This recipe
is just one of many blends.*

TASTING NOTES

Tighten your dentures: it takes time to chomp through this nutty textured combination; muesli
belongs to the 'slow food' movement of another kind. But it's worth being unhurried, as muesli
is full of surprises: just as you're biting into an almond, there's a soft, juicy sultana or a coconut
piece on the next chew. Don't skimp on quality yoghurts and accompaniments – this can make
or break the eating experience. Fresh, tangy berries (blueberries, blackberries, raspberries and
sliced strawberries) add moisture and acidity that counterbalance the dryness and sweetness
of the cereal, while banana provides a creamy, soft foil to the crunchy nuts. Enjoy with a glass
of freshly squeezed OJ and a thick newspaper. ● *by Kate Armstrong*

ORIGINS

The cold, damp climate and poor soil made it difficult to cultivate wheat in ancient Ireland but oats thrived, and when combined with the Irish love of all things dairy, porridge was born. Of course the Scots (and numerous others) also lay claim to inventing this time-honoured dish but whatever its origins, it's a warming, early-morning belly filler, immortalised in fairy tales and beloved by farmers, athletes and health gurus for its simplicity, subtle nutty flavour and slow release of energy.

SERVES 2

IRELAND

PORRIDGE

Possibly the world's oldest bowl food, porridge is a blend
of oats and milk that has transformed itself from gruel
of the impoverished masses to hipster health kick.

YOU'LL NEED
½ cup oats
½ cup milk
1 cup water
pinch of salt
brown sugar

METHOD
1 Place the oats in a pan with the milk, water and salt.

2 Cook slowly over a gentle heat for 5-10 minutes, stirring
regularly to prevent sticking.

3 Ladle into bowls and sprinkle with brown sugar or your
favourite toppings.

TASTING NOTES
A low-fat, low-GI, cholesterol-lowering wonder, you could make a case for porridge as the
original superfood. One of its superpowers: on a winter morning so cold and dark you can
barely force yourself out of bed, it embraces you like a warm blanket and sets you up for
the day. One of its real joys is its versatility, and you can pimp your porridge with any
number of enhancements: honey or maple syrup, cream or Greek yoghurt, blueberries or
banana, stewed fruit, cinnamon, pumpkin or chia seeds. Whether you use rolled oats or
pinhead oatmeal is purely a matter of taste, the only difference is that the finer the oats, the
smoother the texture. ● by Etain O'Carroll

ORIGINS

The introduction of the Amazonian açaí berry to America spawned the trend of the 'superfood smoothie'. Entrepreneurial, health-conscious foodies wanting to make a meal of the smoothie started thickening the mixture with frozen fruits or vegetables so it could be topped with nuts, seeds, fresh fruit and even cereal. Its extremely photogenic appearance took it from fad to phenomenon on image-powered social networks like Instagram and Pinterest. The ubiquitous smoothie bowl was born.

SERVES 2

USA

ZUCCHINI AND FIG SMOOTHIE BOWL

Think of it as a cross between ice cream without the guilt and a wholesome breakfast cereal – a smoothie in a bowl, turbocharged with your choice of yummy toppings.

YOU'LL NEED

2 medium zucchini
   (courgettes), frozen and
   chopped
¼ cup dried figs
½ cup coconut water
2 tbs cashew butter (or
   almond or peanut butter)
¼ tsp ground cinnamon
granola and halved fresh figs,
   to serve

METHOD

1 Blend all of the ingredients except the granola and fresh figs in a blender until smooth.

2 Add more coconut water or cashew butter to achieve the creamy texture of your choice.

3 Serve in a bowl topped with the granola and fresh figs.

TASTING NOTES

It's not like eating a milkshake with a spoon. A classic smoothie bowl has the texture of a dense fruit puree and is more akin to the experience of eating ice cream. Championed by yoga devotees and gym buffs and now found in juice bars and breakfast joints everywhere, a subtly sweet and creamy blend of frozen fruit or vegetables is topped with a carnival of artfully placed chopped fruit (the more exotic the better) and spiked with the crunch of crisp coconut flakes or earthy cacao nibs. The result is an energising, satisfying, nutrient-rich breakfast, or a snack that makes you feel like you've eaten a meal. ● *by Johanna Ashby*

SOUPS

Almost every country has its version of healing chicken soup. Welcome to our chicken soup smack-down, where the world's cuisines go head to head: whose riff on chicken soup is the most consoling? Let the contest begin! But be it chicken or seafood or meat-free, creamy or light, chilli-hot like harira or cool like gazpacho, there's nothing that says comfort like a bowl of soup.

🥣 Easy 🥣 🥣 Medium 🥣 🥣 🥣 Hard

ORIGINS

There is little agreement about the origin of *ajiaco*. Could it be connected to the eponymous Cuban stew, once a typical meal of that island's Taíno indigenous people, who also gave *aji* (hot pepper) its name? (Although note that *ajiacos* of Cuba and Peru are quite different.) Or perhaps it's a variation on a soup of the ancient Colombian Muisca people, cooked with the same local ingredients available today? The jury's out on the backstory, but decidedly in on the tastiness of the result.

TASTING NOTES

Ajiaco has been called a celebration of the Andean home's hearth. More than just a Sunday family favourite, it features several unique Colombian ingredients including three Andean potatoes – the *criolla* (a yellow, nutty-tasting tuber that dissolves into the broth), the *sabanera* (a red/purple-skinned potato) and the *pastusa* (like a small russet). It also features the herb *Galinsoga parviflora*, a weed in much of the world but known locally as *guasca*. Colombians show understandable pride in their nourishing, one-pot meal, with its creamy texture and mix of mild, indigenous flavours, finished with a pleasant bite of capers. *Ajiaco santafereño*, the specialty of Bogotá, is also typically made with chicken. ● *by Ethan Gelber*

SERVES 4

COLOMBIA

AJIACO

A Colombian national dish with Andean flavours, *ajiaco* is a preferred part of holiday repasts, held in particularly high affection by the people of Bogotá.

YOU'LL NEED

2 garlic cloves, minced
2 spring onions (scallions),
   white part only
salt and pepper
2 chicken breasts
4 cups chicken stock
1kg (2lb) *criolla* (or soft yellow
   or white) potatoes, peeled
   and chopped
1 white onion, diced
2 corn cobs, cut in thirds
450g (1lb) *sabanera* (or red)
   potatoes, rinsed, peeled
   and sliced
450g (1lb) *pastusa* (or russet)
   potatoes, rinsed, peeled
   and sliced
2 tbs dried *guasca* (or 1 bunch
   watercress)
1 cup double (heavy) cream
¼ cup capers
2 avocados, pitted and sliced

METHOD

1 Combine the garlic, spring onions, salt and pepper, and then rub the on chicken. Refrigerate overnight.

2 Place the chicken in heavy-bottomed saucepan with stock. Bring to the boil, reduce the heat and cover. Simmer until the chicken is cooked through (about 30 minutes).

3 Remove the chicken and shred into strips. Set aside.

4 Add the *criolla* potatoes to the stock and cook until they disintegrate (about 30 minutes), thickening the soup.

5 Add the remaining garlic, onion, corn, potatoes and *guasca*. Simmer until the potatoes are fork tender (about 45 minutes).

6 Add the shredded chicken and heat until warmed.

7 Top with the dollop of cream, a few capers and the avocado slices.

YOU'LL NEED

1 chicken, 1.5kg (3lb)
1 whole red onion, peeled
1 carrot
½ cup short grain rice
3 eggs
juice of 1 lemon
salt and freshly ground
    pepper, to taste

ORIGINS

Avgolemono, 'egg-lemon' in Greek, describes a number of different soups or sauces using the same technique to create a delicately silky, creamy, tangy result. It's thought that the dish can be traced to Sephardic Jews who brought the recipe to Greece after their expulsion from Spain in 1492. For centuries, they'd been making a similar dish called *agristada* or *salsa blanca*, using verjuice, pomegranate juice or bitter orange juice to sour it; lemon became the Mediterranean's souring agent of choice around the 10th century.

SERVES 6

GREECE

AVGOLEMONO

It's the classic chicken soup of the traditional Greek kitchen. Everyone's favourite dish takes pride of place at Easter, when families come together for the year's biggest feast.

METHOD

1 Rinse the chicken thoroughly and place in a large pot. Add the onion and carrot and fill with enough water to cover by 2cm (1in).

2 Cover and bring to the boil, reduce the heat and simmer for 45 minutes to 1 hour, skimming the fat from the top occasionally. When the chicken is done, the meat should pull from the bones easily.

3 Transfer the chicken to a large bowl. When it's cool enough to handle, pull the meat from the bones and shred it.

4 Strain the broth and remove the onion and carrot. Put it back in the pot and add the rice. Season and simmer for 15 minutes or until tender. Turn off the heat.

5 Whisk the eggs in a large bowl until frothy. Add the lemon juice while whisking.

6 Add one ladle of hot broth into the eggs slowly, while whisking quickly to prevent the eggs from curdling. Gradually whisk in another ladle of broth so the egg mixture is heated.

7 Pour the egg mixture back into the pot, whisking briskly. Season with salt, pepper and lemon juice to taste.

8 Add the chicken meat and serve.

NOTE *Don't let the soup boil once you've added the egg-lemon mixture, or it will break. Reheat leftovers gently without boiling.*

TASTING NOTES

Holy Week – a week of fasting observed by many of Greece's Orthodox Christians – falls after the 40 days of Lent and leads into Easter, the year's biggest feast. On Holy Thursday, eggs are boiled and dyed a deep shade of red, symbolising the blood of Christ. At midnight after the mass of Christ's resurrection on Saturday night, the traditional egg-tapping game is played and *avgolemono* makes its appearance, as the creamy, tangy base to *magiritsa*, the traditional Easter soup. Made with lamb innards – intestines, heart, liver and head, depending on what the family likes best – it uses up the bits of the animal that won't be cooked on a spit later, as the grand finale of the feast on Easter Sunday. ● *by Janine Eberle*

YOU'LL NEED

4 cups water
4 fresh beetroots, scrubbed
2 large potatoes, peeled and
    cubed
½ head of white cabbage,
    chopped thinly
1 yellow onion, peeled and
    chopped
2 carrots, peeled and grated
3 tbs sunflower oil
4 tbs cider vinegar
4 tbs lemon juice
1 tbs brown sugar
¼ tsp salt
6 cups beef stock
2 dried bay leaves
¼ tsp ground black pepper
1 tbs dill, chopped
sour cream or *smetana*,
    to serve

ORIGINS

The great-great-grandfather of
modern borscht was a dish of
humbling simplicity – just a crude
broth made from the pickled
stems, leaves and flowering
umbels of marsh hogweed. The
Ukrainians and Poles probably
have the strongest claims
to being the true fathers of
borscht; the first record of the
dish in Russia came in a 16th-
century homemaking treatise,
which exhorted Russians to turn
their gardens over to hogweed
and share the soup made from it
with the poor.

RUSSIA AND UKRAINE

BORSCHT

SERVES 4

Russia's most famous dish is so much more than cabbage soup; it's a fermented flavour infusion, packed with more vitamins than an athlete's kitbag.

METHOD

1 Fill a large soup pan with the water and boil the beetroots until soft (this may take up to an hour).

2 Remove the beetroots and allow to cool, retaining the water.

3 Peel and slice the beetroots into thin strips.

4 Use the leftover cooking water to boil the potatoes for 15 minutes or so, until soft.

5 After the potatoes have been cooking for 10 minutes, add the cabbage.

6 In a separate pan, fry the onion and grated carrot in oil until soft.

7 Stir the vinegar, lemon juice, sugar and salt into the carrot and onion mixture.

8 Add the beef stock and bay leaves to the pot containing the cabbage and potato.

9 Add the carrot and onion mixture to the cabbage and potato and stir until combined.

10 Add the ground black pepper and chopped dill and stir to combine.

11 Simmer on a medium heat until all the vegetables are cooked.

12 Serve topped with a spoonful of sour cream or *smetana*.

TASTING NOTES

These days, you'll be hard pressed to find borscht made with the traditional hogweed, though it is experiencing a minor resurgence on modern Russian restaurant menus. Instead, the 21st-century version is prepared with fermented beetroot, which gives the dish both its pungent aroma and its vivid, blood-on-the-snow hue. The other ingredients added to this full-flavoured, almost alcoholic base are textures as much as flavours: cabbage, carrot, potato, onions, parsley root, tomatoes, even apples and beans in some more adventurous recipes. And all this with a nutritious beef-bone stock to pack in essential vitamins. The taste of borscht is unmistakably central European: almost beer-like, slightly sour, faintly alkaline, and so obviously packed with nutrients that you can almost feel the goodness flowing into your immune system. ● *by Joe Bindloss*

© FORTYFORKS / SHUTTERSTOCK · © JODIJACOBSON / GETTY IMAGES

ORIGINS

Seder, the ceremonial Passover meal, celebrates the freeing of the Hebrew slaves from Egypt (as told in the Book of Exodus), and much of the food on the Seder table is deeply symbolic. Matzo recalls the unleavened bread the Jews ate as they made their hasty escape – there was no time to wait for the bread to rise. It's thought that the famous dumplings, called *knoedel* or *knoedela* by Ashkenazi Jews in Germany and Poland, were dubbed 'matzo balls' by US vaudeville performers.

YOU'LL NEED

For the stock
1 whole chicken, about 2kg (4lb 4oz)
6 large carrots, peeled and sliced
6 celery sticks, sliced
1 brown onion, skin on, quartered
handful of fresh parsley
handful of fresh dill
2 tsp black peppercorns
2 bay leaves
kosher salt, to taste

For the matzo balls
3 large eggs, beaten
¾ cup matzo meal
¼ cup melted *schmaltz* (chicken fat) or grapeseed oil
½ tsp baking powder
1¼ tsp kosher salt

To assemble
4 small carrots, peeled and diagonally sliced
2 tbs chopped fresh dill
kosher salt and ground black pepper, to taste

TASTING NOTES

Fundamental to the sustaining properties of the soup is the quality of the broth – it should be rich and golden, with the silky mouthfeel of the melted chicken fat that glistens on its surface. About this, there is no argument. Where we get into hot water is the consistency of the matzo balls – the most contested question in all of Jewish cooking. Should they be light and fluffy ('floaters') or dense and chewy ('sinkers')? Each family has their own tradition and their own preference, forged through years, and generations, of celebrating the meal together. Along with matzo ball soup, the Seder meal might include *gefilte* fish (poached fish dumplings), potato *kugel* (a latke-like casserole) and *tzimmes*, a stew of sweet root vegetables and dried fruit. ● *by Janine Eberle*

JEWISH

CHICKEN AND MATZO BALL SOUP

Chicken soup, otherwise known as 'Jewish penicillin', is an unparalleled comfort food credited with quasi-magical healing properties. Served with matzo balls, it forms part of the Jewish calendar's most important celebration.

METHOD

For the stock

1 Cover the chicken with 3L of cold water. Bring to a boil over a medium heat and simmer for 15 minutes, skimming foam from the top.

2 Add all of the other ingredients, reduce the heat and cover (allowing a vent). Simmer for around 2 hours.

3 Remove the chicken from stock and when cool, shred the meat into bite-sized pieces.

4 Strain the stock into a large saucepan – you should have about 2L.

For the matzo balls

1 Combine all of the ingredients in a large bowl (with finely chopped dill if desired).

2 Cover and chill for an hour.

3 Using a spoon or ice-cream scoop, gently roll into 2 tbs–sized balls.

4 Drop carefully, one by one, into a pot of simmering water, cover and simmer until cooked through, 20–25 minutes.

To assemble

1 Bring the chicken stock to a boil, add the carrots and season to taste. Reduce the heat and simmer until the carrots are tender, 5–7 minutes.

2 Add the reserved meat and matzo balls to warm through.

3 Sprinkle with chopped dill and serve.

ORIGINS

Chorba beida, traditionally served during the month of Ramadan, is of uncertain provenance, although rumour has it that its roots lie in Algeria's northeastern cities of Constantine and Annaba. It's said that an elaborate version of the soup, featuring almonds and saffron, was the dish of choice for dignitaries and royalty during major celebrations. It was later adopted by Algeria's middle classes, who replaced the costly nuts and golden stamens with chickpeas, cinnamon and vermicelli.

YOU'LL NEED

1 tbs butter
2 tbs olive oil
1 small free-range chicken, jointed into eight pieces
1 onion, peeled and finely chopped
3 garlic cloves, peeled and crushed
1 tsp ground black pepper
½ tsp chilli flakes
1 tsp ground cinnamon
1 tsp sea salt
400g (14oz) canned chickpeas, drained and rinsed
handful of vermicelli noodles
1 egg yolk
juice of 1 lemon
small bunch of fresh coriander (cilantro), chopped

SERVES 4

ALGERIA

CHORBA BEIDA

White in colour and delicate in flavour, this fragrant chicken soup spiced with cinnamon, lemon and herbs is the best of Algerian home cooking.

METHOD

1 Heat the butter and olive oil in a large heavy-based casserole over a medium heat. Add the chicken and fry until golden, then remove and set aside.

2 Add the onion and cook until soft and translucent, about 15 minutes.

3 Add the garlic, pepper, chilli, cinnamon and salt, and stir for 1 minute.

4 Return the chicken to the pan, add 4 cups water, bring to the boil, then cover and simmer for 30 minutes.

5 Add the chickpeas and vermicelli, and simmer for 15 more minutes. Turn off the heat.

6 Combine the egg yolk and half of the lemon juice in a bowl and beat with a fork until they're well mixed.

7 Slowly add the lemon and egg mixture into the saucepan, whisking briskly to avoid curdling. The soup should turn a creamy white.

8 Divide the soup between four bowls, sprinkle with fresh coriander and add a squeeze of lemon before serving.

TASTING NOTES

The first thing you'll notice about *chorba beida* is its distinctive colour (the name literally means 'white soup'). The second is its delicate flavour, an altogether more subtle experience than its bolder and more brightly coloured sister, *harira*. A perfect *chorba beida* should be light, subtly spiced and velvety in texture, cut through with the sharpness of lemon, and bulked up with toothsome chickpeas and pieces of tender chicken falling off the bone. While its wholesome properties make for an excellent homemade cold remedy, it's perhaps best enjoyed with an Algerian family during Ramadan, alongside a spread of equally enticing dishes, to break the fast of the day. ● *by Nana Luckham*

ORIGINS

The first written recipe for cock-a-leekie soup dates back to 1598 but it's likely that this hearty broth is far older. It's a thrifty dish using up the leftovers from a roast chicken but somehow the result is far greater than the sum of its parts. It's often served on Scottish holidays such as St Andrew's Day, Burns Night or Hogmanay, and in a dubious claim to fame, was featured on the lunch menu of the *Titanic* on the day it sank.

YOU'LL NEED

1 tbs vegetable oil
4 chicken thighs
2 carrots, peeled and
   roughly chopped
2 celery sticks, roughly
   chopped
2 leeks, outer leaves
   removed, chopped into
   rounds
few sprigs of thyme
1 bay leaf
10 stoned prunes
salt and pepper
crusty bread, to serve

SERVES 4

SCOTLAND

COCK-A-LEEKIE SOUP

A profoundly comforting broth of chicken and leeks, this soup
has long been a Scottish favourite and is traditionally served
on a cold winter's evening, when it warms from within.

METHOD

1 Heat the oil in a large saucepan and fry
the chicken thighs until golden brown, then
remove and set aside.

2 Add the carrots, celery and leek to the pan
and fry for 5 minutes.

3 Return the chicken to the pan with the
vegetables and cover with cold water. Add the
thyme and bay leaf and simmer for 1 hour.

4 Remove the chicken with a slotted spoon,
shred the meat from the bones and return it
to the pan.

5 Slice the prunes, add to the pan and simmer
for another 20 minutes.

6 Remove the thyme and bay leaf, season with
salt and pepper and ladle into bowls. Serve
with crusty bread to mop up the broth.

TASTING NOTES

There are few things more satisfying than a bowl of well-made cock-a-leekie soup served
with some crusty bread by a roaring fire, especially at the end of a wet day in the hills or out
at sea. The silky broth is infused with deep layers of flavour, each mouthful merging peppery
soup with succulent chicken, softened leeks and the rich sweetness of prunes. Together
they harbour an almost magical power to restore aching bodies and numbed limbs. After a
day clambering up Scottish peaks and down misty glens, it's a life-saver best eaten with your
boots drying out by the fire, the sound of the wind howling outside and the waves lashing at
the shore. ● *by Etain O'Carroll*

ORIGINS

Legend has it that a beautiful but unhappy bride named Ezo attempted to impress her future mother-in-law by cooking this soup, hence the name *Ezogelin* ('*Ezo*, the bride'). References to red lentil soup and its soothing properties can be found in Turkish medicinal manuscripts, as far back as the 14th century. Prepared with unripe grape juice or vinegar, or even chicken meat, the soup was deemed a cure for everything from headaches to the flu and smallpox.

TURKEY

EZOGELIN ÇORBASI

SERVES 4

This slightly spicy and satisfyingly heart-warming orange-hued lentil soup is a popular and nutritious way to start the day in Turkey, served with hunks of warm *pide* (bread).

YOU'LL NEED

1 tbs butter
1 tsp flour
1 tbs tomato paste
1 tbs red pepper paste (or an equal quantity of additional tomato paste)
1 tbs dried mint
1 tsp red pepper flakes (or an equal quantity of hot paprika), plus extra to serve
1 cup red lentils, washed but not soaked
⅓ cup bulgur wheat
5 cups vegetable stock
lemon wedges, to serve

METHOD

1 Melt the butter in a large pan over a medium heat.

2 Stir in the flour to make a paste.

3 Cook the flour paste, stirring, for 1 minute.

4 Stir in the tomato paste, red pepper paste, dried mint and red pepper flakes.

5 Cook, stirring, for 2 minutes.

6 Add the red lentils, bulgur wheat and stock and bring to the boil.

7 Reduce the heat to low and simmer for 20–30 minutes, stirring occasionally, until the lentils are soft.

8 Serve immediately with a squeeze of lemon and extra red pepper flakes to taste.

TASTING NOTES

As a breakfast item or afternoon snack in Turkey, *Ezogelin çorbası* is light and delicately flavoured with just enough kick from the distinctive red pepper flakes, an indigenous condiment found all over Turkey that is used to season most foods in the same way as salt and pepper are employed elsewhere. The addition of chunks of tomato and other flavourful spices, a popular method of preparing the soup in Anatolia, makes for a hearty and satisfying meal in its own right. Hot from the soup pot, soft lentils and cracked bulgur wheat give an earthy, mealy texture while the quintessential Turkish triumvirate flavourings of dried mint, red pepper paste and red pepper flakes lend the soup a uniquely aromatic and exotic character, which is virtually impossible to replicate with substitute ingredients. ● *by Johanna Ashby*

ORIGINS

It was the breadbasket of the USSR during Soviet times, and Latvia's cuisine has long focused on seasonal produce from its hundreds of freshwater lakes and arable lowlands. Like Latvia itself, this dish is an amalgam of external influences from cultures that once laid claim to the region – German, Swedish, Polish and Russian. The Swedes and Russians introduced vegetable soups (pea and beet respectively); Latvians embellished the recipe with a protein, giving them the energy to work the fields.

YOU'LL NEED

2 tbs oil
1 onion, peeled and finely chopped
2 celery sticks, finely chopped
1 carrot, peeled and finely chopped
½ small fennel, finely chopped
2 garlic cloves, peeled and minced
1 cup dry white wine
1 large tomato, finely chopped
4 cups fish stock
450g (1lb) white river fish fillets
100g (3½oz) crayfish tails
lemon juice, to taste
handful of fresh flat leaf parsley, chopped
handful of fresh dill, chopped

SERVES 4

LATVIA

FISH SOUP

Fish soup is Latvia's best example of real-deal home cooking and seasonal bounty. This version, with hints of New Nordic mastery, is a world away from Soviet-style pork and potatoes.

METHOD

1 Heat the oil in a large pan, add the onion, celery, carrot, fennel and garlic and let them sweat gently until they soften.

2 Add the wine, tomato and stock and bring to the boil, then cover and simmer gently for 30 minutes.

3 Roughly chop the fish fillets, and add them, with the crayfish tails, to the pan.

4 Cover the pan and let the mixture simmer for about 5 minutes (or until the seafood is just cooked).

5 Season to taste with additional salt and pepper, and add a squeeze of lemon to taste.

6 Sprinkle with chopped parsley and dill, and serve in deep bowls.

TASTING NOTES

Latvian fish soup is light and aromatic with an added flourish of dill and parsley that enhances the freshness of the soup's lake fish and (ideally) farm-to-pot veggies. The broth itself is quite clear, allowing for the gentle fish flavours to shine through, unlike other seafood soups such as chowders, which temper the seafood taste with cream. This particular recipe comes from the Dome Hotel in Riga's Old Town, a luxury property set in a restored 13th-century townhouse. Their spin on the Latvian classic takes its cues from the New Nordic trend of elevating traditional homespun dishes into high-end restaurant cuisine. ● *by Brandon Presser*

ORIGINS

Andalusians credit the invention of gazpacho to the Romans, though obviously the Roman version came a few centuries too early to include tomatoes. This proto-gazpacho was most likely conceived as a way to use up stale bread in peasant kitchens, consisting of little more than old crusts, vinegar, water, olive oil and salt. In time, the Romans left and Cordoba and Seville became the de facto home of gazpacho, spawning a host of vegetable variations.

TASTING NOTES

The funny thing about cold soup is that it needs to be eaten when it's hot – about 35°C (95°F) in the shade would do it, ideally on the terrace of an Andalusian villa. Against this baking backdrop, the unlikely combination of stale bread, garlic, olive oil, wine vinegar and fresh-from-the-garden vegetables, pounded together and chilled, is deliciously refreshing. This is the sun-kissed taste of the Mediterranean countryside in a savoury smoothie. Variations abound. In Cádiz, sparse water supplies led to the creation of *arranque roteño*, so thick it could almost be a dip. In Extremadura, hunks of ham are added to the mix. To be truly authentic, any gazpacho should be pounded with a pestle and mortar to release the flavours. ● *by Joe Bindloss*

SERVES 4

SPAIN

GAZPACHO

Like revenge, gazpacho is a dish best served cold; its icy medley of pounded vegetables, vinegar, olive oil and leftover bread is the perfect antidote to the Mediterranean heat.

YOU'LL NEED

2 garlic cloves, peeled and diced

1 red onion, peeled and diced

1 red (bell) pepper, seeded and diced

½ cucumber, diced

500g (1lb 1oz) ripe plum (roma) tomatoes, diced

100g (½oz) stale crusty white bread, broken into small chunks

salt and ground black pepper, to taste

4 tbs olive oil, plus extra for brushing toast

1 cup passata

4 tbs sherry vinegar

1 tsp sugar

toasted crusty white bread, to serve

METHOD

1 Place the diced garlic, onion, pepper, cucumber and tomatoes together in a large bowl.

2 Add the bread and season with salt and pepper, to taste.

3 Add the olive oil, passata, sherry vinegar and sugar.

4 Squeeze the mixture together with your hands to blend the flavours.

5 Cover and place in the fridge overnight to chill.

6 Remove from the fridge and pound the mixture in a pestle and mortar, to make a smooth mix (alternatively, blend in a food processor).

7 Return to the fridge until ready to serve.

8 Present your gazpacho at the table, served with toasted crusty white bread, brushed with olive oil and seasoned with salt and pepper, for dipping.

ORIGINS

In legend, the soup first appeared in 1600s West Africa after Spanish and Portuguese colonists brought groundnuts from South America. The nuts were an ideal thickener when dairy products were difficult to obtain. Today, African-Americans often serve peanut butter soup during the holiday of Kwanzaa between December 26 and January 1 to celebrate the nut's tie to their African roots.

YOU'LL NEED

1 whole chicken, jointed, preferably free range and corn fed
2 medium onions, peeled
salt to taste
1 large, very ripe tomato
1 Scotch bonnet chilli pepper
pinch of cayenne pepper
3cm (1¼in) piece of ginger, peeled and grated
3 tbs peanut butter
1 small glass of water
additional water
omo tuo (rice balls) or *fufu* (pounded cassava), to serve

TASTING NOTES

You're not looking for a bowl of liquid peanut butter; the best groundnut soup is an exercise in subtle nuttiness – deep, rich and enhanced by the zing of Scotch bonnet chillies and an aromatic, tomatoey base. The texture should be silky smooth without descending into sauce-like thickness. Then there's the business of mopping up. Some prefer the dense stickiness of *omo tuo* (balls of pudding rice); others a doughy glob of *fufu* (pounded cassava). Chicken pieces should be firm and on the bone – all the better for dunking and slurping. And forget about cutlery – using your hands is all part of the experience (eat with your right hand please!). ● *by Nana Luckham*

SERVES 4

GHANA

GROUNDNUT SOUP

This spicy soup is traditionally made with roasted groundnuts (peanuts) although peanut butter is commonly used today. Flavoured with ginger, garlic, tomato and chicken, it's your lip-smacking passport to West Africa.

METHOD

1 Put the chicken pieces in a large pan, cast iron if possible.

2 Chop one of the onions and scatter over the chicken along with a pinch of salt.

3 Put the pan on the lowest heat, cover and cook very gently for 15 minutes.

4 Don't chop the remaining onion, the tomato or the Scotch bonnet chilli pepper; instead keep them whole and add them to the pan with the cayenne pepper and grated ginger, then cook gently for 10 more minutes.

5 Meanwhile put the peanut butter in a blender along with the glass of water and whizz to a smooth paste.

6 Pour the peanut paste into the pan and simmer for 10 minutes.

7 Remove the tomato, onion and Scotch bonnet chilli pepper from the pan. Put them in the blender and puree to a smooth paste.

8 Transfer the paste back into the pan, add enough water to just cover the chicken and simmer for 30 minutes. Serve with *omo tuo* or *fufu.*

ORIGINS

Harira's origin dates back centuries in Morocco, with the soup's recipe evolving from family to family. Variations can be as subtle as the inclusion of paprika and cumin, or as strong as the addition of *smen*, a fermented butter with an almost blue-cheese flavour. While most people prefer the consistency to be velvety smooth, some recipes thicken the soup into a stew with rice or broken vermicelli. Its popularity has now spread throughout the Muslim world.

YOU'LL NEED

2 tbs butter
450g (1lb) diced lamb
1½ tsp ground black pepper
1 tsp ground turmeric
1 tsp ground cinnamon
¼ tsp ground ginger
¼ tsp ground cayenne pepper
90g (about one stick) celery, chopped
1 yellow onion, peeled and chopped
1 red onion, peeled and chopped
¼ cup chopped fresh coriander (cilantro)
800g (1¾lb) tomatoes, chopped
6½ cups water
140g (5oz) dried green lentils, rinsed and drained
420g (14oz) canned chickpeas, rinsed and drained
110g (4oz) spaghetti
2 eggs, beaten
juice of 1 lemon

SERVES 6

MOROCCO

HARIRA

Moroccans en masse reach for *harira* to break each fasting day of Ramadan for good reason. This soup, laden with chickpeas, lentils and tomatoes, is as healthy as it is hearty.

METHOD

1 Melt the butter in a large soup pan. Add the diced lamb, black pepper, turmeric, cinnamon, ginger and cayenne, and the chopped celery, onion and coriander and stir frequently for 5 minutes until the lamb is browned.

2 Add the tomatoes and simmer for 15 minutes.

3 Add the water and lentils. Bring to a boil, then reduce the heat. Cover and simmer for 2 hours.

4 Turn the heat to medium-high about 10 minutes prior to serving and add the chickpeas and spaghetti (and more water if the mixture is too thick; it should be velvety).

5 After 10 minutes, stir in the beaten egg and lemon, and cook for an additional minute. The eggs should form white streaks.

6 Remove from the heat and serve.

TASTING NOTES

The daily drama and *halqa* (street theatre) in Djemaa el-Fna, Marrakesh's main square, usually subsides each evening when the countless chefs arrive to start preparing dinner for the thousands, but during Ramadan a different story plays out. Quiet crowds of Moroccans gather round large cooking vats full of *hariria*, each person seemingly counting the seconds till sunset. Even if you'd had a large lunch, the fragrant smells of cinnamon, turmeric and pepper emanating from the soup as it's stirred are enough to make your stomach grumble. When the flood of eating begins, grab a bowl and tuck into this zesty and warming meal. It's traditionally served with crusty bread and eaten with a *taghanjat* (wooden spoon). ● *by Matt Phillips*

YOU'LL NEED

7 tomatoes, whole
230g (8oz) tomatillos, whole
3 medium red (bell) peppers,
  seeded and roughly
  chopped
1 onion, peeled and roughly
  chopped
1 *guaque* chilli
1 *pasilla* chilli
6 Cobán chillies
6 garlic cloves, peeled
4 cups chicken stock
1 tbs annatto-seed paste
1.5kg (3½lb) turkey legs
  (approx 3)
salt and pepper
1 bunch of spring onion
  (scallion) stalks
1 bunch of fresh coriander
  (cilantro), chopped
handful of mint leaves,
  chopped, to garnish

ORIGINS

Kak'ik is the dish time forgot:
unchanged from when the
Q'eqchi' Maya, Guatemala's
largest ethnic group, were
cooking it a millennium back.
Several ingredients, like the
tomatillos and the *guaque/
pasilla* chillies, herald from
the Mexican part of Mayan
civilisation, but true *kak'ik*
concocted in its home (Alta
Verapaz's capital, Cobán) utilises
smoky *chiles cobaneros*
(Cobán chillies).

SERVES 6

GUATEMALA

KAK'IK

This ancestral Mayan turkey, tomatillo and annatto-seed soup is as faithful to pre-Hispanic Latin American cuisine as it gets, the startling red hue evoking the blood of ancient sacrificial rites.

METHOD

1 To make the red sauce: place the tomatoes, tomatillos, red peppers, onion, four cloves of garlic, and the *guaque, pasilla* and Cobán chillies under a hot grill. Cook the vegetables until brown and beginning to char.

2 Blend the browned vegetables and the chillies, thinning the mixture if necessary with a little chicken stock (60ml or ¼ cup). Add the annatto-seed paste and blend again. Strain and set to one side.

3 Put the turkey legs in a pan with enough chicken stock to cover each leg. Add 1 tsp of salt and the remaining two garlic cloves.

4 Cover and cook for about 1 hour on a low-medium heat until the turkey is tender.

5 Add the spring onions and half the coriander to the pan after 30 minutes.

6 When the turkey is cooked, remove the spring onions and add the red sauce. Stir well.

7 Add the rest of the chopped coriander and bring slowly to the boil. Reduce the heat to low-medium, and cook for another 30 minutes, until reduced.

8 Season as desired with salt and pepper. Add mint to garnish.

TASTING NOTES

Visit the rudimentary back-street Mayan kitchens and street-side stalls for the very best *kak'ik*. Preparation begins with the traditional killing, smoking, boiling and plucking of the turkey. Then there's the assembly of the vegetables: the reds (peppers, tomatoes), the greens (tomatillos) and a rainbow of chillies. Cobbled together, the resulting broth should be russet red-orange, achieved by slow roasting and the addition of annatto-seed paste. *Kak'ik* is as hot as its colour suggests. The '*ik*' (spiciness) hits you in a four-flanked attack of the three chillies followed by the pepperiness of the annatto seeds, complementing the citrus tang of the tomatillos. A broth is velvety, with the turkey leg falling off your spoon in softened tomato and chilli-infused morsels. ● *by Luke Waterson*

YOU'LL NEED

1in (2.5cm) piece of fresh
　ginger, chopped
3 garlic cloves, chopped
2 white onions, peeled
　and sliced
2 Scotch bonnet chillies
8 whole tomatoes
450g (1lb) goat or lamb, diced
2 tbs vegetable oil
50g (2oz) tomato puree
4 cups vegetable stock
fufu or *banku*, to serve

ORIGINS

Light soup is a key component
of Ghanaian cuisine. Every
home cook and chef has their
own version, and the fiery
liquor forms the base of other
Ghanaian classics such as
groundnut and palm nut soups.
A classic taste of West Africa,
different countries across the
region have their own much-
loved versions, from Nigeria's
pepper soup, traditionally
made with goat meat, to a less
pungent Sierra Leonean version,
made with fish and served
over rice.

GHANA

LIGHT SOUP

This clear and nourishing broth is comfort food Ghanaian style. Laced with chilli and fragrant ginger and fortified with hunks of lamb or goat, it's a Sunday lunch essential.

METHOD

1 Puree the ginger, garlic, chilli, one onion and half the tomatoes in a blender to form a thick paste.

2 Place the meat in a bowl with the mixture, coat well and marinate for at least an hour, preferably overnight.

3 Heat the vegetable oil over a medium heat in a heavy bottomed pan.

4 Add the meat and its marinade and gently fry for 5 minutes.

5 Add the tomato puree, stock and remaining tomatoes and onion and simmer until the meat is tender (1–2 hours).

6 Remove the onion and tomatoes and puree in the blender, then return to the soup, straining through a sieve.

7 Stir and season to taste.

8 Ladle into bowls, along with a healthy serving of *fufu* or *banku*.

TASTING NOTES

A steaming, aromatic bowl of light soup is a wonderful thing for the senses: bright red in colour, rich and deeply flavoured, with a nose-tingling hit of chilli heat (the uninitiated should have tissues at the ready). A sizeable hunk of *fufu* (pounded cassava) or *banku* (fermented corn and cassava) to soak up the soup is non-negotiable – this is a dish best eaten by hand. While you could sample light soup shoulder-to-shoulder at a roadside 'chop bar' (food shack), its natural habitat is the Ghanaian home, where, come Sunday afternoon, a rich, spicy scent fills the air and the whole family gathers around the table. ● *by Nana Luckham*

YOU'LL NEED

12 medium-size quahog (or other) clams
1 tbs salted butter
2 slices bacon, diced
¾ cup onion, peeled and chopped
2 cups potatoes, peeled and cubed
¼ cup dry white wine
2 sprigs of thyme
1 bay leaf
1 cup double (heavy) cream (or half-and-half)
ground black pepper, to taste
¼ cup chopped parsley
oyster crackers, to serve

ORIGINS

The original New England-style clam chowder probably appeared in north-eastern America with 17th-century French or British settlers. They substituted quahogs (a Native American word for 'clams') for fish in the fish-milk stews common at the time in coastal England and France. The new clam-based potage gained in popularity, appearing on the menu of Ye Olde Union Oyster House (the oldest continuously operating restaurant in the country) by 1836. Plenty of other regional clam chowders have joined the ranks since.

USA

SERVES 4

NEW ENGLAND CLAM CHOWDER

There are many varieties of this soup, but the creamy, briny, New England-accented 'chowdah' – once called 'Yankee Doodle in a kettle' – is the first and most well known. And the best.

METHOD

1 Place clams in large pan, add 2 cups water, cover and put on medium-high heat. Cook until clams open (10–15 minutes). Remove clams from shells, chop into small pieces and set aside. Strain clam broth and set aside.

2 In a clean pan, melt the butter over a medium heat. Add the bacon and fry until it starts to brown (5–7 minutes), then remove.

3 Add the onions to the bacon fat and saute until soft but not brown (5–10 minutes).

4 Stir in the potatoes and the wine. Cook, uncovered, until the wine evaporates and the potatoes start to soften (5–10 minutes).

5 Add the thyme, bay leaf and clam broth to cover. Partly cover and simmer until the potatoes are fork tender (10–15 minutes).

6 Pour in the cream and add the clams and bacon. Add pepper to taste and simmer until hot all the way through – do not allow it to boil. Remove from the heat.

7 Remove the thyme and bay leaf and leave the chowder to sit.

8 When ready to serve, reheat to a simmer. Garnish with chopped parsley and serve with oyster crackers.

TASTING NOTES

The shared characteristic of all clam chowders is the bowl-bound presence of potatoes, onions, flaked pork and, of course, clams. New England clam chowder, however, distinguishes itself by its white colour and thick broth, made possible by the inclusion of milk or cream. (The second-most famous clam chowder is the red, tomato-based, Manhattan-style soup created in the 20th century.) Although available all over the USA, New England clam chowder is a classic Boston bisque and one of Maine's most iconic meals. As such, it is best enjoyed in a coastal seafood shack, where key ingredients come straight out of basins brimming with fresh-caught shellfish and crustaceans. ● *by Ethan Gelber*

ORIGINS

The Nahuatl (Aztec language) word *pozolli* meant 'foam', which forms on the surface when the hominy is ready. Before the Spanish arrived, the Aztec version of *pozole* included the human flesh of sacrifice victims. Thankfully, nowadays it's just pork, chicken or even meat free. Corn maize was sacred to the Aztecs and reserved for special rituals, and the dish is still part of many celebrations today. The dish's patriotism can be seen in its three main varieties: red, white and green, the colours of the Mexican flag.

YOU'LL NEED

260g (9oz) pork ribs
260g (9oz) pork shoulder
½ large onion
2 garlic bulbs, broken into cloves
1 bay leaf
1 tbs salt
2 large chillies, seeds removed
750g (1⅔lb) tinned hominy, drained and rinsed

To garnish

shredded raw cabbage
avocado slices
dried oregano
chilli powder
fresh limes wedges
tostadas (or unflavoured corn chips)

SERVES 4

MEXICO

POZOLE

This broth starts with a simple base of white corn and pork, but lets loose with fresh toppings – radish, avocado, onion, oregano, shredded cabbage – and finishes with festive lashings of chilli and lime.

METHOD

1 Put the pork in a large pan with 3L of water. Bring to a boil and simmer for 10 minutes, skimming the surface with a spoon.

2 Add the onion, garlic cloves, bay leaf and salt. Simmer for 2 hours or until the ribs are tender and can be easily pulled from the bone.

3 Strain and set aside the stock. Pull the pork from the bones, shred roughly and set aside.

4 Blend 1 cup of the stock with the chillies until smooth.

5 Strain the blended mixture into a large pan and add the rest of the stock and the hominy.

6 Simmer for about 30 minutes, or until the hominy expands and begins to soften.

7 Add the shredded pork meat to the pot and gently warm.

8 Serve the *pozole* in deep bowls, and at the table offer cabbage, avocado, oregano, chilli and lime wedges, along with *tostadas*.

TASTING NOTES

The chewy hominy is a blank canvas, but this dish is all about the journey. The broth begins with whispers of cumin and garlic but can end as a riot of flavours. That's because the toppings are presented in separate dishes from which you can build your own perfect bowl. Add a shake of chilli to test your threshold; then add more. Add lime. Too tangy? Drop in some cabbage and avocado slices to smooth things out. Or dip in with tostadas (crispy tortillas). *Pozole* is made for festivities such as Christmas – it's easy to get carried away with too much of this or that, but like opening Christmas presents, this social dish gives everyone the chance show off what they've done with their bowl. ● *by Phillip Tang*

YOU'LL NEED

2 Cornish game hens or other
  small chicken, each around
  450–680g (1–1½lb)
½ cup short grain rice, rinsed
  and soaked for 2 hours
2 fresh ginseng roots, tops
  cut off
2 dried *jujubes* (red dates)
16 garlic cloves
3 spring onions (scallions),
  finely chopped

NOTE Banchan, *or side
dishes, are almost always
served before any Korean
meal. Typical* banchan *include
sukjunamul (marinated mung
been sprouts), ojingeochae
muchim (dried shredded
squid) and of course, the
most famous of Korean foods,*
kimchi *(fermented spicy
vegetables).*

ORIGINS

Traditional Korean culinary
philosophy considers food as
both sustenance and medicine,
and few Korean dishes exemplify
this as clearly as *samgyetang*,
chicken soup made from a whole
bird stuffed with a veritable
apothecary of beneficial roots
and vegetables. In winter, the dish
wards off colds, while in summer
a hot bowl of *samgyetang* is
eaten in accordance with the
Korean nutritional philosophy
of overcoming heat with heat.
Speciality restaurants throughout
Korea serve *samgyetang*
year-round.

SERVES 2

KOREA

SAMGYETANG

Hearty, healthy *samgyetang* (ginseng chicken soup) is a physical tonic, mental stimulant and hangover cure. And as if that weren't enough, it's also reputed to boost the libido.

METHOD

1 Clean the game hens inside and out, removing the giblets and trimming away any visible fat. Rub the outsides with salt then rinse under running water.

2 Rinse the ginseng and *jujubes*. Make shallow cuts into the ginseng root to help release its flavour into the meat.

3 Stuff the cavity of each hen with rice, 8 cloves of garlic, a *jujube* and a ginseng root.

4 Place any leftover rice and garlic cloves in a pan with the hens, and add 8 cups of water.

5 Bring to the boil, cover and cook over medium-high heat for 30 minutes.

6 Lower the heat and simmer for 40 minutes, skimming fat and adding more water if needed.

7 To serve, transfer each hen to an individual bowl, adding broth and garnishing with chopped spring onions.

TASTING NOTES

In Insadong, Seoul's main tourist district, you notice a line of people waiting in the sweltering summer heat outside a restaurant. Inside, people are eating steaming-hot bowls of soup. In the middle of summer? Another patron, sensing your confusion, says '*iyeolchiyeol*' or 'fight fire with fire!'. Soon enough, you're eating a whole young chicken from a hot stone bowl. The broth has a deliciously herbal fragrance, and slicing into the tender chicken releases a whole ginseng root, several cloves of garlic and a fat *jujube* (red date) wrapped inside a small mound of glutinous rice. At the end of your meal (which included ample Korean appetisers) you feel energised, fully sated and, strangely enough, cooler. *Iyeolchiyeol* indeed! ● *by Joshua Samuel Brown*

YOU'LL NEED

1½kg (3lb 3oz) veal shanks
1kg (2lb 2oz) pork belly,
  roughly chopped
1 chicken, around 800g (1¾lb),
  jointed
2 large onions, peeled and
  sliced
3–4 garlic cloves
salt
stale bread

© COLLECTOR / ALAMY, © VICKY SP / SHUTTERSTOCK

ORIGINS

Hundreds of small *impérios*,
little chapels at the centre
of each parish, dot these
volcanic isles. They honour
the Holy Spirit in a tradition
of Catholicism brought to
the region by the Franciscans
some 500 years ago that
remains unchanged today.
Easter celebrations have long
been celebrated by the entire
community congregating at
their local *império* for prayers
and food, requiring dishes – like
this soup – that provide a simple
and cost-efficient way to fill
everyone's bellies.

SERVES 8

AZORES, PORTUGAL

SOPA DO ESPIRITO SANTO

Soup and Catholicism are the cornerstones of Portuguese culture, and *sopa do Espirito Santo* combines the two – a meaty broth served over moist bread during the height of the islands' Easter festivities.

METHOD

1 Wash the meat. In a large pan, heat around 5L (1gal) of water to near boiling.

2 Add all meat, onions and whole garlic cloves and salt to taste.

3 Simmer over a low heat until the meat is tender (around 3 hours), skimming off any scum as necessary.

4 Remove the meat from the soup.

5 To serve, place slices of bread at the bottom of a large soup bowl for each person. Pour soup over the bread and serve the meat on the side with your choice of boiled vegetables.

TASTING NOTES

For the full effect, it's best to ladle out large spoonfuls from a vat, like the locals do on the islands when handing out bowlfuls to their fellow community members on Whit Sunday. Warm slurps nourish the soul as the spring winds tear through the volcanic archipelago. And while all of the Azorean islands are united in their fervent devotion to the Holy Spirit, they each serve the eponymous soup in different ways. On Faial, for example, the soup is served with a heaping side of vegetables. On Terceira the dish appears alongside their signature slow-cooked meat platter *alcatra*, whose spices were brought to the area long ago by Arab and Indian traders. ● *by Brandon Presser*

ORIGINS

Ubiquitous across the Malay Peninsula, *tom yam* is a fiery palate-cleanser that is served everywhere from Thailand and Laos to Malaysia and Singapore. Prawns have been farmed in Thai creeks for centuries, so the dish may have its roots far from the sea, but liberal use of chilli dates *tom yam* to after the 17th century, when the first ones were transported to Southeast Asia from South America by Portuguese seafarers.

YOU'LL NEED

3 cups (750ml) fish or chicken stock
4 garlic cloves, peeled and crushed
5 shallots, peeled and thinly sliced
2 lemongrass stalks, cut into 2.5cm (1in) slices
4 thin galangal slices
200g (7oz) straw mushrooms, sliced lengthways
10 bird's-eye chillies, cut lengthways
3 tbs fish sauce
5 kaffir lime leaves
260g (9oz) raw prawns (shrimp), washed, peeled and de-veined
juice from 1 lime
handful of chopped fresh coriander (cilantro) leaves, to garnish

SERVES 4

THAILAND

TOM YAM GUNG

Take fresh prawns, straw mushrooms and stock, add one part lemongrass, one part lime and one part napalm and serve – Thailand's favourite soup is a chilli-laced masterpiece.

METHOD

1 In a pan or wok, bring the stock to the boil, then add the garlic, shallots, lemongrass and galangal.

2 Add the straw mushrooms, chillies, fish sauce and kaffir lime leaves.

3 Return to the boil for 2–3 minutes, then add the prawns (shrimp) and cook until just done.

4 Remove the pan from the heat and add the lime juice, then stir and serve, garnishing each portion with chopped coriander.

TASTING NOTES

Floating pools of red chilli oil provide the first warning that something fiery lurks beneath the surface of this seafood soup. Vapours of lemongrass, galangal and lime rise up, promising a visceral tour through the flavours of Southeast Asia. The first sensation is the tang of lime but, almost immediately, the chilli takes control. This is a dish to eat quickly, without pausing, in case the fire proves too powerful to quench. The main ingredients – prawns (shrimp) and mushrooms – are secondary to the complex take-no-prisoners blend of spices and seasonings. Each takes its own moment to shine; some spoonfuls dominated by lemongrass and lime, others by chilli and medicinal notes of galangal. Keep tissues to hand... ● *by Joe Bindloss*

SALADS & HEALTHY BOWLS

I t's the go-to health meal of our times – a bowl brimming with quirky grains and a host of fresh, often raw ingredients. You'll find plenty of those here, but also wholesome bowls of goodness with a longer tradition – raw-fish bowls from Japan and Hawaii, classic salads, and flavours from Morocco and China given a modern twist.

Easy Medium Hard

ORIGINS

As far back as the 14th century, Koreans wanting a fresh start and a clear pantry for the lunar new year would combine leftover side dishes from other meals with rice to form *bibimbap*. This complete meal in a bowl also made the perfect shrine offering to ancestors. Although *dolsot bibimbap*, served in a hot stone bowl, may seem traditional, actually it's a recent evolution and before the 1970s, any bowl would do.

TASTING NOTES

It's icy in Seoul and you take shelter in a tiny restaurant, slipping off your shoes. You're presented with a heavy stone bowl containing a kaleidoscope of carrots, shiitake mushrooms, spinach and courgette (zucchini), all perfectly julienned. The race is on to mix it all together while the bowl is hot – wait too long and the raw egg won't cook in the hot rice, and the rice will stick to the bottom. Mixing through the thick red *gochujang* (spicy red pepper paste) and meat means you can control the flavour intensity to your own taste. Crisp radish, juicy bean sprouts, rich beef and fermented soy bean paste keep your tastebuds constantly dancing between excitement and comfort. ● *by Phillip Tang*

SERVES 4

KOREA

BIBIMBAP

A colour wheel of vegetables, spicy red pepper paste, meat and egg make for good looks, but it's the medley of fresh, cooked and fermented flavours that make *bibimbap* a health-bowl star.

YOU'LL NEED

pinch of sugar
1½ tbs soy sauce
¾ cup sesame oil
3 tbs garlic, peeled and crushed
salt and pepper
400g (14oz) beef Scotch fillet, finely sliced into 5cm (2in) strips
1 cup dried shiitake mushrooms, soaked and finely sliced
2 small carrots, peeled and julienned
1 small daikon (or radish), peeled and julienned
2 small courgettes (zucchini), julienned
1 small bunch of spinach
1½ cups bean sprouts
2 cups short or medium grain rice, cooked
4 egg yolks
gochujang (red pepper paste)

METHOD

1 Mix together the sugar, 1 tbs soy sauce, a splash of sesame oil, 3 tsp of garlic and a pinch of pepper. Add the beef and mix well.

2 Stir-fry until the beef is browned, then set aside.

3 Mix together the remaining soy sauce, a splash of sesame oil, 2 tsp of garlic and pepper. Mix in the mushrooms and set aside.

4 Stir-fry the carrot in a splash of sesame oil with 2 tsp of garlic and a pinch of salt and pepper. Set aside.

5 Repeat with the daikon and courgettes (zucchini).

6 Repeat with the bean sprouts.

7 If using ceramic bowls, line the bottom of each bowl with a teaspoon of sesame oil. Put rice in each bowl and arrange small mounds of beef and vegetables over the rice, with an egg yolk in the middle. If using stone bowls, pour another tablespoon of sesame oil around the edge of the bowl and place on the stove to heat on high for 5 minutes, or until you can hear the rice crackle, then remove from the heat.

8 Serve with a dish of *gochujang* for each person to mix into their bowl to taste.

ORIGINS

It's not clear who first reinvented the classic Mexican burrito before the fast casual restaurant boom of the 1990s saw them explode *en masse* on to the scene. But their central premise – take all the favours of the beloved tortilla-wrapped treat and place them into a bowl, thus avoiding both the extra carbs and the risk of sauce squirt – has been embraced ever since. Today they're stalwart of fast-food joints and food trucks, and the often-Instagrammed result of thousands of homemade experimentations.

YOU'LL NEED

1 tbs vegetable oil
4 tsp chipotle paste
2 garlic cloves, peeled and finely chopped
2 tsp ground cumin
½ tsp dried oregano
juice of 2 limes
2 boneless chicken breasts
1 cup long grain rice
1½ cups chicken stock
handful of fresh coriander (cilantro)
salt and pepper, to taste
2 cups shredded lettuce
400g (14oz) canned black beans, rinsed and drained
¾ cup *pico de gallo* (chopped tomato, onion, serrano or jalapeño chilli, coriander (cilantro) and lime juice)
½ cup guacamole
½ cup sour cream
½ cup grated Monterey Jack or Gouda cheese

SERVES 4

USA

BURRITO BOWL

A burrito without the flour tortilla or the mess: think spice-infused meat, grains, beans and whichever toppings you desire, all layered artfully into a bowl.

METHOD

1 Combine the vegetable oil, chipotle paste, garlic, cumin, dried oregano and half the lime juice in a bowl and stir to combine. Add the chicken and marinate for at least an hour.

2 Grill the chicken for 5–6 minutes on each side, or until it is cooked through, then slice it into strips.

3 While the chicken is cooking, put the rice and stock into a pan. Bring to the boil, then simmer, lid on, until the stock is absorbed and the rice is cooked through (about 10 minutes).

4 Stir in the remaining lime juice and chopped coriander, plus salt and pepper to taste.

5 To assemble, divide the lettuce equally among four bowls, followed by the rice, the chopped grilled chicken, black beans, *pico de gallo*, guacamole, sour cream and cheese.

NOTE *Feel free to replace the rice with quinoa or cauliflower rice, substitute fish for chicken, or use yoghurt instead of sour cream.*

TASTING NOTES

Burrito bowls were born in the USA and this is still the best place to try one. Practically every mid-range Tex-Mex chain in the country has its own version – from low-cal bowls of veggie goodness to calorie laden carb-fests slathered in cheese and sour cream – while hipster food trucks pedal ever-more exotic versions, such as *kimchee* and chicken tandoori. The best thing about sitting down to a burrito bowl? The variety of different textures and flavours on offer: cool, tangy sauces, crunchy salad and veggies, tender grilled meat, nutty grains – you name it. Customise as your appetite desires and dig in! ● *by Nana Luckham*

YOU'LL NEED

2 garlic cloves, peeled and
  crushed
⅔ cup olive oil
3 slices of day-old white
  sourdough bread, cut into
  crouton-sized cubes
2 anchovy fillets
1 egg yolk
juice of ½ lemon
2 heads of romaine lettuce,
  torn into rough pieces
handful of finely grated
  parmesan

ORIGINS

Caesar Cardini, the Italian
immigrant credited with
this salad's invention, was
flummoxed on a busy American
Independence Day in 1924
when his kitchen in Tijuana
ran short of ingredients. He
pooled together what he had,
and the original Caesar salad
was born. Anchovies have since
replaced Worcestershire sauce
in most recipes, and the salad
is no longer finger food – it was
designed to be eaten that way,
one leaf at a time.

SERVES 4

TIJUANA, MEXICO

CAESAR SALAD

Salty and tangy, crispy and crunchy, this salad assaults the palate on several fronts – all of them positive. Egg, anchovies and the mighty romaine lettuce provide superfood power.

METHOD

1 Let the garlic infuse in the olive oil for at least an hour.

2 Preheat the oven to 200°C (400°F).

3 Toss the sourdough cubes in a bowl with a little of the oil.

4 Bake for approximately 15 minutes on a tray in the oven until crisp and golden brown.

5 In the salad bowl, mash the anchovies with a fork into a paste.

6 Beat in the egg yolk, before gradually pouring in more of the garlic-infused oil, until it reaches your desired thickness.

7 Finish the dressing by stirring in the lemon juice until smooth.

8 Add the romaine to the salad bowl.

9 Toss well, add the parmesan and then toss again to combine.

10 Top with the croutons and serve.

TASTING NOTES

The salty, tangy and savoury nature of the anchovies permeates the salad, much more so than the original recipe's simple use of Worcestershire sauce. The sharpness of the lemon, and the richness from the parmesan add a depth to the flavour, while the crunch of the garlic-infused sourdough croutons makes the perfect accompaniment to the moist, crisp romaine. From its humble, if accidental, beginnings in Tijuana, this salad has spread around the globe, and is now found everywhere from New York to London and Sydney. Grilled chicken is often offered as an optional topping, as are capers and bacon. ● *by Matt Phillips*

YOU'LL NEED

1 red onion, peeled and thinly
   sliced
1kg (2lb 2oz) fillets of fresh firm
   white fish (eg sea bass) cut into
   large bite-sized chunks
1 pinch of red chilli flakes
3 garlic cloves, peeled and finely
   chopped
½ cup fresh lime juice
3 tbs olive oil
2 tsp rice vinegar
¼ tsp caster (superfine) sugar
1 Peruvian *aji limo* chilli, seeded
   and chopped (substitute a
   small red chilli if not available)
2 corn cobs, cut in half
2 sweet potatoes, peeled and
   sliced thinly
3 tbs chopped fresh coriander
   (cilantro) leaves
salt
ground black pepper

ORIGINS

The roots of *ceviche* go back
to Incan times when *chicha*, a
marinated corn drink, was used
to flavour fish prior to cooking.
The lime was introduced to
Latin America by Spanish
conquistadores, proving a
sublime match for the white fish
of South America's Pacific coast.
Some also believe that ocean-
going navigators from Polynesian
islands introduced a version of
the dish to Easter Island and
continental South America.
Dishes such as Rarotonga's *ika
mata* are very similar.

SERVES 6 AS A STARTER

PACIFIC COAST, PERU

CEVICHE

Combining a Spanish-influenced citrus and coriander (cilantro) punch with marinated raw fish and chillies used in Incan times, Peru's national dish has now been adopted and adapted across Latin America.

METHOD

1 Layer half of the sliced onions in a glass bowl and lay the fish on top. Sprinkle on the chilli flakes and chopped garlic and cover with lime juice.

2 Cover the bowl and place in a refrigerator to marinate for 2 hours. During this time spoon the lime juice over the fish two more times.

3 Whisk together 2 tbs of the oil, the rice vinegar and caster sugar until smooth, then add the chopped fresh chilli.

4 After the fish has been marinated, drain and discard the lime juice and stir in the mixture of oil/rice vinegar/caster sugar/chilli, blending well.

5 Preheat a grill to medium.

6 Brush the corn and sweet potato with the remaining oil and place under the grill for 10–15 minutes, turning frequently until cooked and lightly charred.

7 Divide the *ceviche* into six servings. Top with chopped coriander and the remaining sliced red onion, and season to taste with salt and ground black pepper.

8 Serve with the grilled corn and sweet potato.

TASTING NOTES

On a continent where food can be heavy with carbs – rice, beans and potatoes anyone? – the lightness of flavour of *ceviche* is a revelation. Visually, it's also a diverse treat with red and green accents of chilli and coriander (cilantro) standing out on the neutral canvas of white fish punctuated by the pink of sliced red onion. Your first mouthful will boldly announce the super-fresh crunch of the onions and the sharp punch of lime juice. Then the chilli fire hits, but it's balanced with the freshness of the fish and a subtle sweetness from a touch of sugar, creating an exciting epicurean experience like no other. ● *by Brett Atkinson*

ORIGINS

Never mind the rarity of salads in China, enterprising US chefs have nonetheless christened this celebrity favourite in homage to its Chinese restaurant origins. Madame Wu's Garden Restaurant in Santa Monica is generally credited with inventing the dish for Cary Grant in the 1960s. Its popularity has skyrocketed thanks to chef Wolfgang Puck's version, served at his restaurant, Chinois, and to recipes created by the salad's army of Hollywood devotees, such as Gwyneth Paltrow.

YOU'LL NEED

2 tbs soy sauce
2 tbs sesame oil
2 tbs lime juice
1 tsp sugar
1 tsp grated fresh ginger
salt and pepper, to taste
½ head medium lettuce, finely shredded, plus 2 whole leaves for serving
¼ head cabbage, finely shredded
¼ head radicchio, finely shredded

1 medium carrot, peeled and sliced into thin strips
1 small capsicum, sliced into thin strips
1 cup shredded roast chicken
1 tbs roasted cashews
1 cup crispy chow mein noodles (or omit for a healthier version)
1 spring onion (scallion), diced
handful of chopped coriander (cilantro), to garnish
sesame seeds, to garnish

SERVES 2

USA

CHINESE CHICKEN SALAD

Despite the name, this is a thoroughly American invention and health nut's dream – a light yet satisfying salad packed with addictive crunch and lip-smacking umami.

METHOD

1 For the dressing, whisk together the soy sauce, sesame oil, lime juice, sugar and grated ginger. Season to taste and set aside.

2 Combine all the other ingredients (except the coriander and sesame seeds) in a large bowl and mix well. Add the dressing and toss until all of the ingredients are fully coated.

3 To serve, line the bowls with whole lettuce leaves. Spoon the salad into the bowls and garnish with coriander and sesame seeds.

TASTING NOTES

Crisp lettuce, poached or grilled chicken, a crunchy fried topping and a classic Asian soy and sesame dressing are the hallmarks of a Chinese chicken salad. Variations abound, including a retro version with tinned orange segments and sliced almonds and a more filling one with Chinese cabbage and deep-fried egg noodles. Found on menus everywhere across America, from fast casual chains to upmarket restaurants, this healthy salad is popular for a reason. Each mouthful is the perfect blend of crunchy, salty, sour and sweet, able to satisfy the deepest umami craving. A true one-bowl wonder, it is also one of the few salads that successfully marry eastern and western flavours in one dish. ● *by Johanna Ashby*

YOU'LL NEED

300g (10½oz) short grain rice
⅓ cup sushi vinegar
450g (1lb) assorted sashimi-
    grade fish (tuna, salmon or
    mackerel; if unavailable,
    substitute lightly poached
    prawns (shrimp) or octopus)
nori (seaweed) flakes
sushi soy sauce
wasabi

ORIGINS

Chirashi has its origins in the
Japanese passion for raw fish.
Though *chirashi* is on the menu
at nearly any sushi restaurant, an
increasing number of non-sushi
places serve it alongside simpler
noodle and rice dishes. While
preparing sushi and sashimi
requires years of training, a good
chirashi chef needs only fresh
fish, quality rice and apprentice-
level slicing and rice-making
skills. Restaurants specialising
in *chirashi* often allow diners to
chose their own toppings using
a mix-and-match approach.

JAPAN

CHIRASHI SUSHI

SERVES 4

Japanese for 'scattered sushi', *chirashizushi* (or simply *chirashi*) is blue-collar counterpart to more artisanal sushi varieties. An East Asian comfort dish, *chirashi* prioritises flavour and convenience over dainty presentation.

METHOD

For the rice

1 Rinse the rice thoroughly and repeat 3–5 times until the water no longer runs cloudy.

2 Soak the rice in cold water for 30 minutes, then let it drain for 30 minutes.

3 Place the rice and 390ml (13fl oz) of cold water in a pan, bring to boil, then reduce the heat to low and cook, covered, for 15–20 minutes.

4 Remove the pan from the stove and allow the rice to sit, covered, for 15 minutes.

5 Transfer the rice to a wooden bowl; slowly fold in the sushi vinegar with a wooden spoon.

For the fish

1 Ensure your workspace and hands are impeccably sanitary.

2 Slice the fish into thin slices of around 2–4cm (1–1½in), or small cubes of 1cm³ (½in³).

3 Place the prepared rice into bowls and carefully arrange slices or cubes of fish on top.

4 Garnish with nori flakes and serve with soy sauce and wasabi on the side.

TASTING NOTES

Wandering through Tokyo, you find yourself before a humble-seeming restaurant whose main splashes of colour come from slabs of fish behind a chilled glass counter. Sitting next to a man dressed in a crumpled suit, you point discreetly at his wooden bowl filled with rice and vivid fish slices and say to the server, '*Are o kudasai*' ('I'll have that, please'). Moments later, you're served a bowl of warm vinegar-scented rice topped with three generously proportioned slices each of tuna, salmon, mackerel and octopus, garnished with flying fish roe and a single large shrimp (head still on). Though hardly fancy, the fish is sparkling fresh, and the meal both filling and tasty. Unpretentious *chirashi* – sushi for grown-ups. ● *by Joshua Samuel Brown*

ORIGINS

The Hollywood Brown Derby Restaurant, a mecca for Tinseltown celebrities in the 1930s, is credited with the invention of the Cobb salad. Its owner, Robert Cobb, in search of a midnight snack, raided the fridge to make an impromptu bowl of cold chicken, bacon, hard-boiled egg, avocado, tomato, lettuce and blue cheese with French vinaigrette. A chance tasting so impressed a customer that it was soon added to the restaurant's menu, quickly becoming its signature dish.

YOU'LL NEED

3 tbs olive oil
1 tbs red wine vinegar
1 tsp Dijon mustard
1 tsp lemon juice
½ tsp Worcestershire sauce
¼ tsp sugar
1 small garlic clove, peeled and minced
½ head iceberg lettuce, shredded
1 small head gem lettuce, shredded
1 cup grilled chicken breast, finely cubed
2 strips bacon, fried and chopped
2 hard-boiled eggs, diced into small cubes
2 medium red tomatoes, diced into small cubes
50g (2oz) blue cheese, crumbled
1 avocado, pitted and diced into small cubes
snipped chives, to garnish

SERVES 2

HOLLYWOOD, USA

COBB SALAD

This tried-and-true classic has both glamour
and substance, proving chopped salad can
be a meal on its own and look good, too.

METHOD

1 Make the dressing by whisking together
the olive oil, vinegar, mustard, lemon juice,
Worcestershire sauce, sugar and garlic in a
bowl. Set aside.

2 To assemble the salad, place the lettuce in
a wide bowl and top with the chicken, bacon,
eggs, tomatoes, blue cheese and avocado in
neat, vertical rows.

3 Sprinkle with snipped chives and serve with
dressing on the side.

NOTE *For optimal presentation, chop the
salad ingredients into equally bite-sized
pieces.*

TASTING NOTES

Despite its origins, a good Cobb salad is definitely not an opportunity to clear out the
fridge but a carefully crafted combination of sweet, salty, sour, bitter, soft and crunchy
elements that are more than just an afterthought. Easily identifiable with its neat, colourful
rows of brightly coloured ingredients, its universal appeal is down to the classic flavours of
salty bacon with juicy chicken, tangy tomato and crisp lettuce, creamy avocado and sharp
vinaigrette. As American as baseball and apple pie, Cobb salad is considered an integral
part of a home cook's repertoire and it seems no stateside restaurant menu is complete
without it. ● *by Johanna Ashby*

YOU'LL NEED

1 stale pita, split into two
2 ripe tomatoes, cut into
    chunks
2 small cucumbers, roughly
    diced
6 radishes, quartered
2 spring onions (scallions),
    sliced
¼ cup coarsely chopped
    flat leaf parsley,
¼ cup coarsely chopped
    fresh mint
bunch of purslane (optional)

For the dressing

2 garlic cloves, peeled
    and crushed
⅓ cup extra virgin olive oil
juice of ½ a lemon
3 tsp pomegranate molasses
1 tsp sumac
salt and ground pepper,
    to taste

ORIGINS

Welcome to the Levant,
a swathe of the eastern
Mediterranean including Israel,
Jordan, Lebanon, Palestine,
Syria and Turkey. One of many
shared culinary traditions is
the eating of flatbreads, and
fattoush developed as a way to
use up stale leftovers. Another
distinctively Levantine touch
is the use of sumac, the dried,
ground berries of a bush that
grows wild here. The spice was
used to add a lemony flavour
before actual lemons became
widely spread in the region
around 1000 AD.

SERVES 2

LEBANON AND SYRIA

FATTOUSH

This refreshing salad, crunchy with radish and cucumber, zingy with lemon and pomegranate molasses, is ubiquitous in the countries of the Levant, where it forms a vital part of the *mezze* table.

METHOD

1 Heat the oven to 180°C (350°F). Separate the pita into two rounds, and bake for 5–7 minutes, until very crisp but not browned.

2 For the dressing, whisk together the garlic, olive oil, lemon juice, pomegranate molasses, sumac, salt and pepper in a small bowl, and leave to infuse.

3 Combine the vegetables and herbs in a large bowl and toss well.

4 Just before serving, give the dressing a quick whisk, pour it over the salad and toss.

5 Top the salad with the toasted pita and an extra sprinkling of sumac. Serve immediately in big bowls, and eat while the pita is still crisp.

NOTE *Purslane, a wild green, is traditional but may be hard to find. If you want a salad with more leafy heft, use romaine lettuce in its place.*

TASTING NOTES

When you visit the countries of the Levant, your introduction to *fattoush* is likely to be as part of *mezze*: a banquet of small dishes, hot and cold, consumed at a leisurely pace and often accompanied by *arak*, an anise-flavoured spirit similar to Greek *ouzo*. As the feast is delivered to your table dish by dish, you may encounter old friends such as hummus, *tabbouleh* and *baba ghanouj*; and make some new ones: *kibbeh*, fried balls of cracked wheat and minced meat; *kibbeh nayyeh*, the Lebanese version of steak tartare; and *sambousek*, fried pastries filled with lamb or cheese. *Fattoush* acts as a tangy palate cleanser among the variety of the *mezze* table, its cool cucumber and lip-smacking lemon resetting your tastebuds for the next delicious mouthful. ● *by Janine Eberle*

ORIGINS

Horiatiki in Greek translates to `peasant salad`, so it's safe to assume the origins are rural in nature. The salad's essential ingredients are believed to be what farmers would bring to the fields for their snack, though it's thought they would keep the constituents whole and bite straight into each item separately. This eventually evolved into the mixed salad we see today, complete with a sprinkling of oregano and trickle of olive oil and vinegar.

SERVES 4

GREECE

HORIATIKI (GREEK SALAD)

The Greek salad has plenty of pretenders, but the original
is the *horiatiki*. As simple as it is full of fresh flavours,
it screams of the Mediterranean and summer.

YOU'LL NEED

- 2 green (bell) peppers, seeded and roughly chopped
- 1 large cucumber, peeled and roughly chopped
- 1 small red onion, peeled and diced
- 5 ripe tomatoes, roughly chopped
- 340g (12oz) Kalamata olives, pitted
- 140g (5oz) Greek feta
- 1 tsp dried oregano
- 3–4 tbs extra virgin olive oil
- 3–4 tbs red wine vinegar

METHOD

1 Place the chopped ingredients in a large bowl with the olives.

2 Crumble the feta over the mixture, followed by a sprinkling of oregano, olive oil and red wine vinegar.

3 Mix well and serve immediately.

TASTING NOTES

The summer sun is shining down and you're having a lazy lunch in a Greek taverna by the sea (preferably with your toes in the sand). The coolness of *horiatiki* cuts through the heat, and the variety of tastes in it blend brilliantly: the sweetness of the tomatoes, the slight bitterness of the green (bell) peppers, the saltiness of the feta, the sharpness of the red onion and cleansing nature of the cucumber. ● *by Matt Phillips*

ORIGINS

Every Friday lunchtime, Moroccan families gather at a low round table with a large platter of couscous before them. It's piled into a pyramid shape around the meat inside, studded with vegetables and topped with a marmalade of spiced raisins and sauce. For special events such as weddings, it's embellished with dried fruit and nuts. Our modern twist on this staple is a feast for the eyes and can be served with any grilled vegetable or meat.

YOU'LL NEED

1–2 eggplants, sliced
salt and pepper
4 tbs olive oil
2 spring onions (scallions), sliced
1 small garlic clove, peeled and crushed with a little salt
1 tsp ground cinnamon
1 tsp ground cumin
1 tsp ground coriander
½ tsp ground ginger
1 heaped tbs raisins
1 tbsp dried apricots, chopped
2 tsp runny honey
1 cup vegetable stock
140g (5oz) couscous
1 heaped tbs fresh pomegranate seeds
1 tbs pine nuts, toasted
1 fresh fig, chopped
handful of coriander (cilantro) and mint leaves, chopped

SERVES 2

MOROCCO

JEWELLED COUSCOUS WITH EGGPLANT

Transform humble couscous into a bejewelled beauty, bursting with the fruit and spices that make Moroccan cuisine memorable. Topped with glossy grilled eggplant, it's as pleasing to the eye as it is to the tastebuds.

METHOD

1 Sprinkle the eggplant slices with salt and leave in a colander to drain.

2 Add 2 tbs olive oil to a pan over a medium heat and add the onions, garlic, spices, raisins, apricots and honey. Stir gently for 3 minutes.

3 Add the stock and bring to the boil.

4 Add the couscous, stir to mix, cover and turn off the heat. Cover and let sit for 5–10 minutes.

5 Wash the salt off the eggplant and pat dry.

6 Brush the eggplant with 2 tbs olive oil and season with salt and pepper.

7 Grill for about 5 minutes per side until browned, brushing with more oil as necessary.

8 Fluff up the couscous with a fork, taste and season with salt and pepper. Stir in the pomegranate seeds, pine nuts, fig, coriander and mint leaves.

9 Serve the couscous in bowls with the grilled eggplant slices on top.

TASTING NOTES

Wander through any Moroccan souk and you'll soon come across a spice merchant. He'll have colourful piles of ground spices, whole cloves, black peppercorns, fresh turmeric, saffron and nutmeg, as well as dried rosebuds, lavender and thyme. Moroccan cuisine is all about spicing. It's never searingly hot, and always an interesting blend of flavours: think cinnamon, cumin and ginger, with bursts of freshness from mint and coriander (cilantro) leaves. It also marries sweet and savoury – here we have onions, garlic, spices and herbs mingling with a dash of honey and sweet fruits such as fresh figs, dried apricots, raisins and pomegranate seeds. With the added crunch of toasted pine nuts, these are the perfect ingredients to brighten the tiny grain-like pasta that is couscous. ● *by Helen Ranger*

AUVERGNE, FRANCE

LE PUY LENTIL SALAD

SERVES 2

Praised locally as 'vegetarian caviar', Le Puy lentils grow only in the volcanic soil of France's Auvergne. This vitamin-packed pulse, adored by chefs, makes a deliciously nutty bowl salad.

YOU'LL NEED

3 tbs good-quality olive oil
2 shallots, peeled and finely chopped
1 carrot, peeled and julienned
2 garlic cloves, peeled and crushed
3 cups vegetable stock
340g (12oz) Le Puy lentils
1 sprig of thyme
1½ tbs white wine vinegar
½ tsp mustard
pinch of salt and pepper

METHOD

1 Heat 1 tbs of the olive oil in a large pan over medium heat. Add the shallots and sweat for a couple of minutes.

2 Add the carrots and cook for a few minutes, then add the garlic, stir and reduce the heat to low.

3 Pour in the vegetable stock and add the lentils and thyme, and simmer gently for 15–20 minutes, until the lentils are firm – they should retain some bite and not be too soft.

4 Drain excess liquid using a sieve and transfer the lentils into a large bowl.

5 To prepare the dressing, pour the remaining olive oil, vinegar, mustard and a pinch of salt into a glass jar, screw on the lid and shake vigorously. Drizzle over the lentils and toss.

6 To serve, heap into two bowls and add a sprinkling of pepper.

TASTING NOTES

The town most strongly associated with these superfood lentils is Le Puy-en-Velay, and most gourmands enjoy their first forkful amid the merry din of a local restaurant. With brick walls and rough-hewn wooden tables, traditional restaurants are numerous around Rue Pannessac, and while the atmosphere is casual, regional produce is prepared with reverence. Sturdy *cuisine paysanne* (peasant cuisine), such as coarse sausages and stews, is laid out on checked tablecloths with a flourish – and usually a side dish of expertly cooked Le Puy lentils. When seasoned just right, Le Puy lentils form the main course: a bowlful of firm, grey-green gems, studded with carrots and laced with a tart vinaigrette to offset the lentils' nutty flavour and discreet sweetness. ● *by Anita Isalska*

ORIGINS

Archaeological digs tell us that humans have consumed mussels for thousands of years, and given the fact that this delectable treat grows in abundance (and is considered to be underutilised), it may be around to feed us for millennia more. It's no surprise that the grape-loving French were the ones to transform the mussel into a delicacy with wine, and it was such a hit that *moules marinières'* popularity quickly outgrew France's borders.

YOU'LL NEED

2kg (4lb 4oz) fresh mussels
100g (3½oz) unsalted butter, cubed
4 French shallots, peeled and diced
1¼ cups dry white wine
4 sprigs of thyme, leaves picked
2 bay leaves
bunch of flat leaf parsley, chopped finely
salt and ground black pepper, to taste
French baguette, to serve

TASTING NOTES

There's a bit of a chill on, with the wind blowing off the English Channel. Stepping into an atmospheric eatery with a roaring fire may start to thaw your extremities, but the best cure to warm your insides is a steaming bowl of *moules marinières*. The gorgeous freshness of the mussels in combination with the subtle sweetness of the shallots and the acidic dry white wine is soothing on so many levels. Many recipes also call for cream, which mellows the flavours but adds richness to the sauce. There's no need for utensils – simply use one of the empty shells as a pincer to pluck the lovely morsels from the other mussels. Mopping up the sauce with a fresh French baguette is only icing on the proverbial cake. ● *by Matt Phillips*

NORMANDY, FRANCE

MOULES MARINIÈRES

Superfood meets fast food. Yes, really. This classic dish from Normandy may take humble mussels to a higher level, but it won't take you long to get them there.

METHOD

1 Rinse the mussels in running cold water before scraping off any barnacles or dirt. Don't scrub them as this may cause the shells' colour to leach out during cooking, turning the juice an unappetising shade of grey. You'll need to throw away any with broken shells. If any are open, give them a sharp tap: if they remain open, you'll need to bin them too.

2 Remove the little fibrous beards (the appendages that the mussels use to attach themselves to the rocks) by pulling them sharply towards each mussel's hinge. Let the mussels sit in cold water for a couple hours

3 Melt the butter in a large pan. Add the diced shallots and cook for 8–10 minutes until translucent in colour.

4 Add the wine and bring to a simmer. Reduce the heat and cook the shallots gently for a further 5 minutes.

5 Drain the mussels.

6 Turn up the heat to medium-high, then add the mussels as well as the thyme and bay leaves. Cover and cook for around 3 minutes (until most mussels have opened).

7 Add the parsley and give the pan a good shake to mix.

8 Remove any mussels that are still closed.

9 Season lightly and serve straightaway in a bowl, together with the liquid.

TIP *The freshness of the mussels is paramount. A fresh mussel is tightly closed, heavy with seawater and shiny. There should be no fishy smell.*

ORIGINS

Well before the term 'superfood' was a buzzword and healthy eating became a lifestyle brand, London-based chef and writer Yottam Ottolenghi was extolling the virtues of vegetables without excluding meat. Championing ingredients both unglamorous and exotic, such as eggplant, cauliflower and sumac, Ottolenghi's signature style of complex flavours, colourful dishes and above all, always tasty food undeniably changed the British food scene, just as Julia Child brought home-cooked French cuisine to America.

YOU'LL NEED

1 large cauliflower, trimmed
  and split into florets
2 tbs olive oil
1 tbs sumac
1 tbs *za'atar*
salt
1 cup bulgur wheat
½ cup buttermilk
juice of ½ a lemon
1 tbs pomegranate molasses,
  plus extra for drizzling
2 celery sticks, sliced thinly
  crosswise
½ cup dried dates, chopped
¼ cup pomegranate seeds
1 cup mixed soft herbs such
  as dill, mint and parsley
warm pita, to serve
1 tomato, thinly sliced

LONDON, UK

PERSIAN SPICED CAULIFLOWER AND BULGUR SALAD

SERVES 4

An intellectual feast for the eyes and the tastebuds, this Middle Eastern-inspired salad is a playground of unusual ingredients and vivid flavours.

METHOD

1 In a large bowl, mix the cauliflower florets, 1 tbs of the olive oil, sumac and za'atar with your hands, making sure each floret is coated evenly with the oil and spices.

2 Heat the remaining oil in a grill or frying pan. Without crowding the pan, fry the cauliflower in batches, turning the florets every few minutes until they are golden brown on all sides.

3 Set the fried cauliflower aside on paper towels and season with salt.

4 Cook the bulgur according to packet instructions and set aside.

5 To make the dressing, whisk together the buttermilk, lemon juice and pomegranate molasses in a large bowl. Season to taste.

6 Add the cauliflower, bulgur, celery, dates, pomegranate seeds and herbs to the bowl and toss well.

7 To serve, line each of four bowls with three small pita wedges, add the salad and top with the tomato slices and a drizzle of pomegranate molasses.

TASTING NOTES

Authentic Middle Eastern recipes can evoke fear among even competent home cooks, dreading the demands of an ingredients list that might include hard-to-find items such as kohlrabi or Iranian limes. Those who persevere, however, are rewarded with dinner-party impressive and simply delicious dishes. Humble vegetables such as celeriac and broccoli are magically transformed by an array of spices and herbs into an explosion of contrasting yet harmonious flavours – moreish, zesty and satisfying. Best of all, these dishes are often just as good straight from the stove or at room temperature, making them perfect for just about any occasion, from sit-down meals and office lunches to alfresco dining and picnics. ● *by Johanna Ashby*

ORIGINS

From a Hawaiian word meaning to section or slice, *poke* (pronounced poke-ay) was created by fishermen seeking to make a tasty snack from the offcuts of their catch. With its Japanese influence evident in the rawness of the fish and *shoyu* seasoning, the traditional version included native sea algae and candlenuts. *Ahi poke*, the most popular version, is made with tuna, but an average grocery store in Hawaii might offer 10 different versions, from octopus with ponzu dressing to salmon with avocado and sesame oil.

YOU'LL NEED

1 cup short grain rice
6–8 radishes
white vinegar
½ tsp salt
½ tsp sugar
30g (1oz) dried wakame (or use prepared seaweed salad)
340g (12oz) sashimi-grade salmon and/or tuna
1 tbs *shoyu*
sesame oil
1 spring onion (scallion), finely sliced
½ cup shelled edamame
pickled ginger (optional)
½ avocado, thinly sliced
2 tsp white or black sesame seeds, or a mix
2 tsp fried onions

SERVES 2

HAWAII, USA

POKE

A simple salad of marinated raw fish, found everywhere in Hawaii from surf shacks to gas stations, has conquered the world's hip lunch spots in the guise of a gorgeously healthy bowl meal.

METHOD

1 Cook the rice using the absorption method or in a rice cooker, and set aside.

2 Quick-pickle the radishes by slicing very thinly (on a mandoline if possible) and placing in a small bowl with enough white vinegar to cover and mix with the salt and sugar. Let it sit for 15 minutes.

3 Cover the wakame with boiling water and leave to soften, about 10 minutes. Drain, squeeze out excess water, and coarsely chop.

4 Cut the fish into 1cm (½in) cubes. Mix with the *shoyu*, a few drops of sesame oil and the spring onion, and let sit for 5 minutes.

5 To assemble, place some rice in a bowl and place the marinated fish in one corner. Arrange the wakame, edamame, pickled radish and ginger, and avocado around the bowl. Sprinkle with sesame seeds and fried onions, and serve with additional *shoyu* on the side.

TASTING NOTES

New-school *poke*, served everywhere from Boulder to Paris in bright modern canteens and from food trucks, is hard to beat as a healthy lunch on the run, and its versatility means plenty of enjoyable experimentation to find your perfect *poke* groove. Steamed rice is the standard base but quinoa, brown rice and even kale (for the carb-avoiding) are possible. Toss the fish in *shoyu*, add sesame oil or chilli, or use ponzu for a citrus kick. When it comes to toppings, customisation is key – your aim is to hit the right mix of crunchy and chewy, earthy and bright, creamy and acidic. Treat our list as a suggestion – you might add pineapple or mango, sliced cucumber or red onion, wasabi peas or crushed peanuts. Let your imagination, and your tastebuds, be your guide. ● *by Janine Eberle*

YOU'LL NEED

3 tbs sesame seeds
1 tbs sugar
1 tbs soy sauce
2 cups mixed leafy greens
   such as kale, spinach or
   Swiss chard
handful of green beans,
   trimmed
salt and coarse pepper
1 cup short grain rice, cooked
300g (10½oz) firm tofu, diced
1 spring onion (scallion),
   green part chopped finely,
   to garnish

ORIGINS

Shojin ryori is vegetarian cuisine at its purest, practised by the Buddhist monks of Japan from as early as the 6th century. Similar food philosophies are found in the Chinese and the Koreans traditions – they likely introduced the religion to Japan. The traditions of *shojin ryori* echo Zen principles, such as eating in silence or using only what is available. Over time, some of the techniques and skills have evolved to give rise to other forms of cuisine, including the most sophisticated Japanese form of fine dining known as *kaiseki*.

JAPAN

SESAME TOFU BUDDHA BOWL

SERVES 2

With this simple and nourishing yet tasty dish, Buddhist vegetarian cuisine leaves your belly, mind and conscience feeling good.

METHOD

1 In a small frying pan, toast the sesame seeds gently, being careful not to burn them.

2 Transfer the sesame seeds into a mortar and pestle, add the sugar and grind into a paste.

3 Combine the sesame seed paste with the soy sauce in a small bowl and set aside.

4 Simmer the vegetables in a shallow pan with just enough water to cook them without burning. Season to taste.

5 To serve, put some rice in a bowl and top with the vegetables, tofu and sesame sauce. Garnish with spring onion.

TASTING NOTES

The principles of *shojin ryori* are rooted in simple cooking, minimal seasoning and avoiding waste. The result is vegetables that taste of their quintessence without the distraction of sauces or seasonings. A special occasion experience is to try *shojin ryori* cuisine in the *omakase*, or 'chef's choice', style in one of the few remaining specialist restaurants in Kyoto or Tokyo. You can expect the freshest seasonal produce cooked to sublime perfection and served in beautifully adorned, often handmade tableware over multiple courses. These days, a Buddha bowl is also used to describe a vegetarian grain bowl filled with a hearty mound of wholesome, nourishing food, said to resemble the belly of Buddha. ● *by Johanna Ashby*

ORIGINS

Legend has it that *solterito* is named 'little single man' for being an easy-to-make, one-bowl meal for lonesome bachelors – or any singles wanting to get into shape and perhaps change their solo status. It usually appears on Peruvian menus as a cold side dish. But every second Sunday in February, its hometown of Arequipa hosts a festival – *Día del Solterito de queso* – to give this simple but beloved chopped salad the recognition it deserves as a complete feast for all lovers of healthy eating.

YOU'LL NEED

1 cup broad (fava) beans (fresh or frozen)
½ cup diced red onion
1 cup diced tomato
1 cup giant kernel corn, boiled (or substitute yellow corn)
1 cup *queso fresco,* cut into small cubes (or substitute feta)
¼ cup diced *rocoto* (or substitute other red chilli or capsicum)
3 tbs olive oil
3 tbs white or red wine vinegar
salt and pepper, to taste
smoked salmon, thinly sliced, or cooked prawns (optional)
¼ cup black olives, sliced
2 tbs chopped parsley

SERVES 2

AREQUIPA, PERU

SOLTERITO

A salad of giant corn, fava beans, Andean cheese, hot red peppers and olives, born in a Peruvian city dominated by volcanoes, is vibrant enough to hold its own.

METHOD

1 Boil the broad (fava) beans until tender, about 5 minutes. Strain and peel.

2 In a large bowl, mix together the beans, onion, tomato, corn, cheese and *rocoto*.

3 Dress with the olive oil, vinegar, salt and pepper to taste.

4 Add the seafood (if using) and olives.

5 Serve in bowls sprinkled with chopped parsley.

TASTING NOTES

Arequipa is a base for trekkers and condor spotters. At the end of a long morning, you'll inevitably drift into a family-run restaurant with a wobbly ceiling fan, and start the lunch menu with *solterito*. After the stark beauty of canyons and Arequipa's white volcanic-rock churches, a bowl of *solterito* is a chromatic treat – sweet red tomatoes, green broad (fava) beans and purple onion. The salty white Andean cheese (*queso fresco*), and black olives get your mouth watering immediately; the onion and fierce glow of the *rocoto* chilli really start it buzzing. The beans work their buttery charm to calm down the flavours, bringing in the wholesome corn. Rounding this dish out with smoked salmon or cooked prawns (shrimp) makes a meal of it and introduces a *ceviche* vibe. ● *by Phillip Tang*

ORIGINS

One of the first cereals to be domesticated and sometimes called 'the mother of all wheat', *farro* has been found in the tombs of Egyptian kings and is said to have graced the ration bags of Roman legions. It's still grown in mountainous areas of Tuscany (it thrives in barren, high-altitude terrain), where it has long been an essential part of the rustic regional cuisine. Since the 1990s, with its adoption by trend-setting restaurants such as Chez Panisse in California, *farro* has become one of the food world's hippest grains.

YOU'LL NEED

4 courgettes (zucchini), cut into chunks
2 fennel bulbs, trimmed and thickly sliced
1 red onion, peeled and cut into wedges
2 red (bell) peppers, seeded and cut into chunks
2 eggplants, cut into chunks
6 garlic cloves
extra virgin olive oil
sea salt
freshly ground black pepper
2 sprigs of thyme
1 sprig of rosemary
1 cup chopped fresh herbs (parsley, basil, mint, oregano)
300g (10½oz) *farro* (or substitute barley or brown rice)
juice of 1 lemon
feta or goat's cheese (optional)

SERVES 4

ITALY

SUMMER FARRO SALAD

With its hearty, chewy texture and elegant, nutty flavour, this ancient grain forms a tasty platform for a salad bursting with colourful summer vegetables.

METHOD

1 Preheat the oven to 200°C (400°F). Put all the vegetables and 4 whole garlic cloves into a large roasting tray and toss together with a good splash of olive oil. Spread out in one layer and season with salt and pepper.

2 Roast for 30–40 minutes, shaking the tray occasionally, until the vegetables are cooked through and crisp around the edges.

3 Meanwhile, in a medium pan, combine 2 garlic cloves (peeled and lightly crushed), thyme, rosemary and 2 tsp salt with 6⅓ cups water and bring to a boil.

4 Stir in the *farro* and simmer until just tender, about 15 minutes. Drain well, transfer to a bowl and discard the garlic and herbs.

5 Add the chunky roasted vegetables and chopped herbs to the *farro*, dress with olive oil and lemon juice, and season with salt and pepper.

6 Scatter with crumbled feta or goat's cheese and serve in deep bowls.

TASTING NOTES

Lacking the heaviness of many whole-wheat grains, *farro* has a more elegant taste, complex and nutty with undertones of oats and barley. It's not spelt, but spelt's cousin; indeed, wheat taxonomy, complicated by regional naming differences, can leave ancient grain shoppers bamboozled. What is *farro*, exactly? The wheat variety emmer is most common in Italy; when it's grown in the Garfagnana region of Tuscany it can be designated as *farro Indicazione Geografica Protetta*, guaranteeing its origin by law. Look for light-brown, cleft grains with subtle white stripes. And go for a semipearled (*semiperlato*) variety, where part of the bran has been removed, to avoid long soaking or cooking while retaining a good dose of the grain's beneficial fibre, magnesium and vitamins A, B, C and E. ● *by Janine Eberle*

YOU'LL NEED

2–3 medium summer squash
  or courgettes (zucchini)
4 slices of prosciutto or
  bacon
1 medium garlic clove, peeled
  and minced
2 tbs extra virgin olive oil
¼ cup gluten-free
  breadcrumbs
100g (3½oz) goat's cheese,
  roughly chopped
zest of 1 lemon
handful of mint leaves, torn
  into small pieces

ORIGINS

For the illusion of pasta without
the attendant carb-loading, we
have the spiralizer to thank. This
Japanese invention automated
the labour-intensive art of the
garnish known as *mukimono* –
think of the shredded daikon
that graces the world's sushi
platters. A kitchen gadget that
has launched a trend (as well as
a host of unlikely new words),
the spiralizer's popularity has,
er, spiralled steadily upwards,
as Western dieters go gaga over
zoodles (zucchini noodles),
swoodles (sweet potato) or even
coodles (carrot).

SERVES 2

USA

SUMMER SQUASH 'SPAGHETTI'

This gluten-free, carb-free 'spaghetti' with toasted garlic crumb, goat's cheese, lemon and mint may be a far cry from the real thing, but it's just as tasty, and a lighter alternative to pasta.

METHOD

1 Make the 'spaghetti' by using a spiralizer (if you don't have one, you can grate it lengthways in long strokes using the largest holes of a box grater).

2 Fry the prosciutto or bacon in a large frying pan until crisp, then set aside.

3 Blanch the 'spaghetti' for about 2 minutes in a large pan of boiling water, then drain.

4 Warm the olive oil in the frying pan and saute the garlic until fragrant. Add the breadcrumbs and fry until golden brown.

5 Add the cooked 'spaghetti', goat's cheese and lemon zest to the pan and cook until the cheese melts.

6 To serve, put the mixture in bowls, top with crispy prosciutto and garnish with mint leaves.

TASTING NOTES

Ready-to-cook spiralized vegetables running the gamut from beetroot (beet) and pumpkin to apples and pears are increasingly available in organic supermarkets across the USA. Moreover, traditionally the preserve of home cooks, spiralized dishes have now started appearing in American restaurant menus. While vegetable noodles are no substitute for the comforting chewiness of good old-fashioned pasta, what they lack in toothsomeness they make up for with their fresh taste and diet friendliness. The mild flavour and robust texture of courgette (zucchini) or summer squash stands up particularly well to traditional pasta sauces, meaning that not only are they a perfectly acceptable substitute when that pasta craving hits, but a tasty and satisfying way to get more of your five-a-day. ● *by Johanna Ashby*

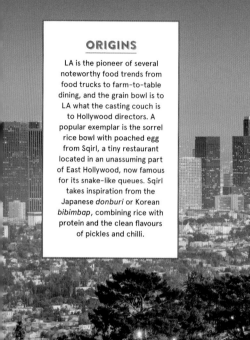

ORIGINS

LA is the pioneer of several noteworthy food trends from food trucks to farm-to-table dining, and the grain bowl is to LA what the casting couch is to Hollywood directors. A popular exemplar is the sorrel rice bowl with poached egg from Sqirl, a tiny restaurant located in an unassuming part of East Hollywood, now famous for its snake-like queues. Sqirl takes inspiration from the Japanese *donburi* or Korean *bibimbap*, combining rice with protein and the clean flavours of pickles and chilli.

YOU'LL NEED

1 chicken breast, sliced crosswise into two
1 tbs olive oil, plus extra for sauteeing
2 lemons
1 garlic clove, peeled and minced
pinch of sea salt
2 tbs plain yoghurt
1 tsp miso paste
1 cup brown rice
1 head broccoli, broken into florets
1 bunch Swiss chard, roughly chopped
1 medium carrot, peeled and chopped into bite-sized pieces
2 tbs butter
1 tbs *umeboshi* plum, seeded and roughly chopped
small handful of tarragon leaves, finely chopped
hot sauce and a squeeze of lemon, to serve

TASTING NOTES

No self-respecting food joint in Los Angeles worth their soft glowing Edison light bulbs and communal tables would be without a grain bowl on the menu. From health-conscious celebrities to Hollywood power lunchers, grain bowls are the ultimate meal catering for those who want variety, flavour and nutrition in a single dish. A perfectly balanced grain bowl will consist of a seasoned grain base, crunchy vegetables and meaty protein lifted by tart, refreshing pickles, a squeeze of acid from citrus and an invigorating hot sauce. Each component should taste good on its own as well as in combination with any one or more of the other elements. ● *by Johanna Ashby*

SERVES 2

LOS ANGELES, USA

TARRAGON GRILLED CHICKEN GRAIN BOWL

This indulgent version of the ubiquitous grain bowl is inspired by trendsetting LA restaurant, Sqirl – a satisfying and visual feast with the perfect blend of grain, vegetables, protein and unifying condiments.

METHOD

1 Prepare the chicken by marinating it in 1 tbs olive oil, the juice from half a lemon, garlic and sea salt. Set aside.

2 To make the dressing, combine the yoghurt, miso paste and juice from half a lemon. Set aside.

3 Cook the rice according to the packet instructions.

4 Saute the broccoli florets in olive oil and a little water until tender, then set aside.

5 Saute the carrots in a small knob of butter until tender, season to taste and set aside.

6 In the same pan, saute the Swiss chard in a little olive oil until wilted and season to taste. Set aside.

7 On a hot grill pan, sear the chicken slices, turning every so often for even colour on both sides, until cooked through. Slice into thin strips and set aside.

8 Prepare the rice by tossing with the remaining butter, *umeboshi* plum and tarragon, adding hot sauce and lemon juice to taste.

9 To serve, smear a dollop of dressing in each bowl, add some rice and top with the chicken and vegetables in neat rows.

10 Garnish with a final squeeze of lemon and mix well before eating.

NOTE Umeboshi *plum is available in Japanese or Asian supermarkets, or substitute preserved lemon or pickled peppers.*

YOU'LL NEED

110g (4oz) black quinoa, rinsed
2 tbs canola or peanut oil
2 tbs fresh ginger, peeled and
  minced
230g (8oz) tempeh, cubed
110–140g (4–5oz) kale,
  chopped
1 chilli, chopped (or dried
  chilli flakes, to taste)
juice of ½ lemon

ORIGINS

This dish is a relatively
modern invention, given that
its constituent ingredients
couldn't come together without
globalised trade and culinary
trends. To be fair, tempeh
is from Indonesia and the
Dutch love *boerenkool* (curly
kale), and a history of Dutch
colonialism *could* have brought
the two ingredients together.
But throwing South American
quinoa into the mix is a distinctly
21st-century innovation, and it's
the sort of combination
that bespeaks a marked Pacific
Rim origination.

SERVES 2

CALIFORNIA, USA

TEMPEH WITH SPICY KALE AND BLACK QUINOA

If superfoods were weather patterns, this dish ploughs straight into a perfect storm – the leafy goodness of kale, the firm earthy bite of tempeh, the comforting starchiness of quinoa.

METHOD

1 Put the quinoa in a pan, cover with water and bring to the boil.

2 Stir, then reduce the heat to medium and simmer for 15 minutes, until the quinoa is cooked but still retains some firmness.

3 In a deep pan, heat the oil over a medium-high heat.

4 Add the ginger and tempeh to the oil. Cook for about 1 minute until the tempeh sizzles and starts to turn brown.

5 Add the kale, chilli and cooked quinoa. Stir-fry for about 5–7 minutes, until the kale has cooked a little, but has not totally wilted.

6 Add the lemon juice.

TASTING NOTES

Black quinoa and tempeh have strong notes of *terroir* – these are earthy ingredients, their solid musk cut by a hint of sweetness. Combined with kale's verdant bitterness, this dish, minus any spicy heat, is surprisingly hearty, if not heavy. But throw in some fire and this recipe takes on a whole new aspect. Fresh chillies add a fruity heat element that lightens the package, while dried chilli flakes are more one-dimensional, but still nicely undercut the soily sweet and bitter base. A little ginger provides a nice refreshing zing, as does a squeeze of lemon juice. If you'd rather add some *umami* (pleasant savoury taste) depth, toss in a dash of *nuoc mam* (fish sauce). ● *by Adam Karlin*

ORIGINS

The ultra-exclusive Waldorf Hotel was newly opened in 1893 when it held its first event, a charity ball. On the menu was Waldorf salad – sliced apple and celery in a mayonnaise dressing – invented for the occasion by the *maître d'hôtel*. Ever since, its simplicity has encouraged innovation; chopped walnuts and grapes or raisins quickly became standard additions, and variations on the theme include Emerald salad, which sees the role of celery usurped by cauliflower.

SERVES 2

NEW YORK CITY, USA

WALDORF SALAD

Invented for the elite, Waldorf has become a favourite salad of the masses. With a classic collection of flavours and textures, this light and refreshing dish makes a perfect bowl for summer.

YOU'LL NEED

140g (5oz) red or green grapes
1 lemon
olive oil
salt and pepper
½ cup walnuts
¼ cup yoghurt
¼ cup mayonnaise
½ tsp mild mustard
1 large, crisp apple
4 celery sticks, leaves
   reserved
shredded chicken; poached
   or hot-smoked salmon
   (optional)

METHOD

1 Preheat oven to 180°C (350°F). Place the grapes on a baking tray, finely grate over the zest of ½ a lemon, drizzle with a little oil and season with salt and pepper.

2 Place in the oven for 15 minutes, then add the walnuts for a further 5–10 minutes, until the grapes are caramelised and the walnuts are golden.

3 Meanwhile, make the dressing. Whisk the yoghurt, mayonnaise and mustard together, squeeze in a little lemon juice and mix well. Season to taste.

4 Finely slice the celery sticks and leaves and cut the apple into large matchsticks. Place into a large bowl and add the walnuts (and chicken or fish if using). Drizzle over the yoghurt dressing and toss well. Scatter the caramelized grapes on top and serve.

TASTING NOTES

This salad is all about the crunch. Crispy apple, celery and roasted walnuts each provide their own brand of bite to this veritable workout for the jaws. The original 100% mayonnaise dressing can be modified (or replaced) with yoghurt for a lighter, more tangy result, and the sweet grapes, oven-roasted with lemon zest, write a new page in this adventure tale of contrasting tastes. (Some recipes rewrite the book completely with the addition of mini-marshmallows – we don't recommend it.) Adding shredded chicken or hot-smoked salmon can make a modest but delicious salad into a bowl-filling meal; a fresh herb such as dill or chervil or some peppery salad leaves will add a different dimension. Don't be shy – this is a salad with a proud history of customisation. ● *by Janine Eberle*

ORIGINS

The emergence of bowl food as 'the new salad' in New York most certainly stemmed from its enthusiastic adoption by upscale salad chains and juice bars. A modern phenomenon, it nevertheless finds its roots in the principles of the macrobiotic diet that burst on to the food scene of the 1960s, encouraging not just healthy food choices but a positive mental outlook and an active lifestyle. Time-poor and wellness-obsessed New Yorkers embraced these wholesome qualities and inspired a social media movement.

SERVES 2

NEW YORK CITY, USA

WILD RICE AND SWEET POTATO POWER BOWL

Nary a lettuce or empty calorie in sight, this New York power salad energises and nourishes with every tasty bite.

YOU'LL NEED

1 sweet potato, peeled and diced

2 tbs olive oil

1 cup wild rice

salt and pepper

1 medium avocado, pitted

juice of 1 lime

1 small garlic clove, peeled and minced

½ cup canned chickpeas

1 bunch of radishes, trimmed and thinly sliced

1 bunch of watercress, trimmed

1 cup roast chicken (optional)

2 tbs sunflower seeds

METHOD

1 Preheat the oven to 200°C (400°F).

2 Spread the sweet potato on a rimmed baking sheet, drizzle with 1 tbs of olive oil and season with salt and pepper. Bake in the oven for 20 minutes or until soft.

3 Cook the rice according to the packet instructions until just tender, then set aside.

4 To make the dressing, combine the avocado, lime juice, garlic and remaining olive oil in a small bowl. Whisk in a little water to thin the dressing to your desired consistency, and season with salt and pepper.

5 To serve, put some rice in a bowl, top with the sweet potato and remaining ingredients and drizzle generously with the avocado dressing.

TASTING NOTES

One of the world's most dynamic and diverse food cities, New York is home to a staggering concentration of eating destinations, including a proliferation of chain and, more recently, pop-up establishments specialising in healthy bowl meals. A classic New York power bowl is a well-balanced blend of grains, vegetables and lean proteins, as well as a tasty way to eat local, sustainable and seasonal ingredients. No longer the domain solely of salad bars, power bowls are everywhere and the variety is seemingly endless, from burrito bowls to meat and three veg. Unsurprisingly, they're particularly popular with city workers and exercise devotees looking for nutritious, filling and novel options for breakfast, brunch and lunch. ● *by Johanna Ashby*

RICE, PASTA & NOODLES

There's something about refined carbs and big bowls that creates the perfect moment of gluttonous comfort. A rainy night in with a bowl of 'spag bol' (that's *tagliatelle al ragù*, actually), a late brunch of Vietnamese pho after a big night out, the feeling of contentment after a feed of mac 'n' cheese or *nasi goreng* – there may be some guilt afterwards, but these are bowls that just make us feel good.

🥣 Easy 🥣 🥣 Medium 🥣 🥣 🥣 Hard

ORIGINS

The Chinese, colonisers of Vietnam for 1000 years from 111 BC, introduced rice cultivation and rice noodles, which developed into the thread-fine rice vermicelli we know today as *bun*. The model *bun* dish is *bun thit nuong*, a bowl of cold *bun* topped with grilled pork. Other varieties include beef (*bun bo nuong*), prawns (shrimp – *bun tom nuong*) and tofu (*bun thit nuong chay*). In Hanoi, the famous *bun cha* allows you to self-assemble your bowl from meatballs, noodles, herbs and *nuoc cham* served separately.

TASTING NOTES

Let your nose follow the street-stall smoke signals to find the aromatic barbecuing meat, and pull up a little plastic stool. As waves of scooters honk by, contemplate the bowl of contrasts you've just been handed – the chicken still sizzles with juice, chilled out with cucumber, lettuce and mint. The carrots thread through crunches of freshness. A springy white bed of cold vermicelli noodles provides the balance – eat more if it gets too spicy or salty. You'll get a separate dish of *nuoc cham* dressing. Pour it all into your bowl (in south Vietnam), or dip slices of meat and prawn (shrimp) spring rolls into it (in the north). This magic liquid ties everything together, the *umami*-rich fish sauce gently wrestling the lime and chilli, making your bowl a juicy, delicious mess. ● *by Phillip Tang*

VIETNAM

BUN GA NUONG

SERVES 2

Juicy charred lemongrass chicken on a bed of cold vermicelli noodles, peppery herbs, cucumber and a sweet fish sauce dressing – the boldest and brightest flavours of Vietnamese cuisine.

YOU'LL NEED

1 garlic clove, peeled and minced
6 spring onions (scallions), finely chopped
1 lemongrass stick (white part only), finely chopped
salt and pepper
vegetable oil
2 chicken breasts
2 blocks dried rice vermicelli
½ iceberg lettuce, shredded
½ cucumber, sliced
¼ cup roughly chopped fresh mint
¼ cup unsalted roasted peanuts, crushed

Nuoc cham dressing

¼ cup water
juice of ½ lime
2 tbs fish sauce
1 tbs sugar
½ tsp peeled chopped garlic
½ tsp chopped fresh chilli
½ cucumber, julienned
½ carrot, peeled and julienned
½ daikon (optional), peeled and julienned

METHOD

1 Place the garlic, spring onions, lemongrass, salt and pepper and vegetable oil in a bowl, and mix together. Add the chicken breasts and leave to marinate for at least an hour.

2 Mix together all the dressing ingredients and set aside.

3 Soak the vermicelli noodles in a bowl of hot water until just soft, about 5 minutes. Drain, rinse in cold water and set aside.

4 Grill the chicken pieces on both sides for about 10 minutes, or until cooked through. Cut into thin slices.

5 Line two deep bowls with lettuce and cucumber slices. Top with vermicelli noodles and chicken. Sprinkle with fresh mint and peanuts.

6 Serve the dressing in individual small bowls for each person to gradually pour over their vermicelli and chicken to taste.

ORIGINS

In Chinese days of yore, street vendors carried their kitchens in baskets hanging on *dan dan* – bamboo poles slung across their shoulders. At the request of hungry passers-by, this could be unharnessed and used to prepare a fast-food noodle feast. The unique spicy-nutty noodle concoction soon became known as *dan dan* noodles, which translates as 'peddler's noodles'.

YOU'LL NEED

300g (10½oz) fresh egg noodles
2 garlic cloves, peeled
5cm (2in) piece of fresh root ginger, peeled
3 spring onions (scallions), white and green parts
2 tbs peanut or canola oil
200g (7oz) minced fatty pork (or beef)
1 tbs Shaoxing Chinese rice wine
salt
handful of dry-roasted peanuts, roughly chopped

Sauce

3 tsp water
2 tbs light soy sauce
3 tbs tahini or sesame paste
1 tbs Chinese black rice vinegar
2–3 tbs chilli oil (adjust for chilli hit)
2 tsp sesame oil
1 tsp sugar
1 tsp ground Sichuan pepper

TASTING NOTES

Sichuan restaurants are sweat-inducing places packed with punters and bubbling bowls of chilli concoctions. Take a deep breath. Locals like to see a foreigner reeling after a mouthful of their native food, in which case *dan dan* noodles is a good option. Its mid-range spiciness is right on the money, with the different textures of noodles, meat and sauce contributing to varying levels of heat. The punch to watch for is the Sichuan pepper. It creeps up on the palate like a tourist to a panda, creating a tingling or anaesthetised *ma-la* sensation, which is as addictive as the chilli hit. Seeing red? Water won't help – the only answer is to keep slurping. ● *by Penny Watson*

SERVES 2

CHINA

DAN DAN NOODLES

This Sichuan dish comprises yellow egg noodles tossed in a red chilli, Sichuan pepper and sesame sauce, topped with minced pork (or beef) fried with aromatics, and finished with peanuts.

METHOD

1 Bring a large pan of lightly salted water to the boil.

2 Cook the noodles for 3–5 minutes until al dente.

3 Rinse under cold water, then drain and tip into a serving dish.

4 In a small bowl, whisk together all the sauce ingredients until combined.

5 Pour the sauce over the noodles and toss. Set aside.

6 In a mortar, pound the garlic, ginger and 2 of the spring onions.

7 Heat the oil in a frying pan over a medium-high heat. Add the garlic, ginger and spring onion paste and fry briefly until fragrant.

Add the meat and stir-fry until it is no longer pink and the pan gets sticky.

8 Deglaze with rice wine and season with salt.

9 Spoon the cooked meat mixture over the noodles, sprinkle with remaining chopped spring onion and the peanuts. Serve straight away.

ORIGINS

The origin of these thin, springy wheat noodles is generally thought to be China. However, down the centuries rāmen has become a cornerstone of Japanese cuisine and there's a vast range of ways to serve the noodles, either in a soupy stock or dry with dipping sauce. In fact, rāmen has developed an international cult following, with chefs vying to prepare unique recipes, including *gekikara*.

YOU'LL NEED

8½ cups chicken stock
4 garlic cloves, smashed
4cm (1½in) root ginger, sliced
1 leek, chopped
1 carrot, peeled and chopped
1 piece of kombu
1 tsp white pepper
2 tbsp soy sauce
2 tbsp mirin (cooking sake)
2 tbsp white sugar
½ cup *gochujang* paste/hot
   pepper paste
1–2 tbsp chilli oil, to taste
450g (1lb) rāmen noodles
2 hard-boiled eggs, halved
pickled bamboo shoots, nori
   sheets, black sesame seeds
   and sliced spring onions
   (scallions), to garnish

SERVES 4

JAPAN

GEKIKARA RĀMEN

Gekikara translates from Japanese as 'hellishly spicy'. Slurping
these noodles, the broth brimming with chilli and pepper, may be
like ingesting molten lava, but it's also a curiously addictive experience.

METHOD

1 Put the stock in a pan. Add the garlic, ginger,
leek, carrot, kombu and white pepper and
bring to the boil.

2 Add the soy, mirin, sugar, *gochujang* and
chilli oil, then reduce the heat and simmer for
15 minutes. Remove the kombu, then cook for
a further hour. Strain and discard the solids.

3 Boil the noodles in plenty of water until al
dente and divide between four bowls.

4 Top with half an egg, bamboo shoots, nori,
sesame seeds and spring onions, then ladle
the spicy soup over the top to serve.

TASTING NOTES

Rāmen bars specialising in this dish often make it available in gradations of spiciness, from
temporarily tongue numbing to off the radioactive scale. The chef will freshly prepare the
dish for you, ladling the fiery red stock, perhaps with an extra dash of chilli oil or generous
dose of pepper powder, over the noodles. Then it'll be topped with garnishes such as bean
sprouts, julienned spring onions (scallions), boiled egg and slices of pork. Follow fellow diners
by slurping the rāmen noisily while eating, with napkin at the ready to dab your perspiring
brow. Despite the feeling of a volcano about to erupt in your belly, don't linger over your
bowl: rāmen is eat-and-go food of the fastest order. ● *by Simon Richmond*

YOU'LL NEED

1kg (2lb 2oz) beef chuck roast, cut into 4 chunks

salt

3 tbs peanut or canola oil

1 tsp Chinese five spice powder

8 garlic cloves, peeled and finely chopped

2cm (¾in) piece of fresh ginger, peeled and sliced

5 spring onions (scallions), cut crosswise

4 dried star anise

2–4 tbs Sichuan peppercorns

3–4 red chillies, split lengthwise

4 tbs chilli bean sauce

4 tbs rice wine

6 tbs light soy sauce

2 tbs dark soy sauce

5 cups water

1 bok choy, cut into large chunks

450g (1lb) thick Chinese egg noodles

ORIGINS

You'll find 'beef noodle soup' throughout Asia, but Taiwan has made this dish its own by localising the ingredients and spicing it up several notches. Beef consumption wasn't big here before 1949 so it's likely the recipe was brought to the island by mainlanders fleeing China's civil war. Spicy stewed-beef noodle soup has existed in China since the Tang Dynasty (AD 618–906). It was popularised by members of the Hui, a Chinese Muslim ethnic group known for hand-pulled noodles.

SERVES 6

TAIWAN

HONG SHAO NIU ROU MIAN

A feature on the Asian must-visit culinary map, Taiwanese dishes aren't generally renowned for their incendiary spiciness. This slow-cooked pot of blistering beefy broth with noodles may just change that.

METHOD

1 Season the beef with salt. Heat the oil in a pan, add the beef and sear it on both sides.

2 Add all remaining soup ingredients, except for the bok choy and noodles. Bring to a boil, skimming fat from the top as necessary. Lower the heat and simmer for about 2 hours.

3 Take the soup off the heat and uncover the pan to allow the steam to evaporate and the broth to become more concentrated as it cools.

4 When the broth has cooled, remove the meat and set it aside.

5 Strain the broth into another pan, discarding any solids, then reheat the broth over a medium heat.

6 Cut the meat into 1cm- (½in-) thick pieces before returning it to broth. Add the bok choy.

7 Cook the noodles in a separate pan of water until they reach your desired texture. Strain and place in individual bowls.

8 Ladle over the broth, meat and bok choy, and serve.

TASTING NOTES

So readily available is this dish in Taiwan that most take its complexity for granted. However, as any chef will attest, making good spicy beef noodle soup is complex and time consuming. Is it worth it? Yes! The secret lies in the process of heating and cooling, allowing the broth to concentrate a very diverse list of ingredients into a unified, spicy – and uniquely Taiwanese – flavour. Good spicy beef noodle soup tempts the tongue without burning it, the anise and five spice offering a rich, savoury counterpoint to the fiery Sichuanese chillies. The beef is flavoursome and tender enough to pull apart with chopsticks, and is often served with chilli-infused dark vinegar mixed with soy sauce. ● *by Joshua Samuel Brown*

YOU'LL NEED

1.5kg (3½ lb) bone-in, skin-on
  chicken thighs
salt
ground black pepper
2 tbs vegetable oil
2 large onions, peeled and
  finely chopped
2 garlic cloves, peeled and
  minced
1 tbs fresh ginger, peeled and
  minced
½ tsp chilli powder
1 tsp ground cumin
2 medium tomatoes, peeled
  and chopped
2 tbs plain yoghurt
½ teaspoon ground
  cardamom
1 cinnamon stick

For the rice

450g (1lb) basmati rice
2½ tbs vegetable oil
1 large onion, peeled and
  diced
5 cardamom pods
3 cloves
1 cinnamon stick
½ tsp ground ginger
4 cups chicken stock
1 pinch saffron, crushed and
  soaked in 1 tbs warm water
coriander (cilantro) leaves and
  fried onions (optional)
dahi or yoghurt, to serve

ORIGINS

Biryani's beginnings are
contested ground. Mentions of
'mutton rice' in Tamil literature
go back to 348 BC, but it's
thought that the dish we know
today originated in India's
Mughal era, brought from Persia
by the Muslim conquerors
who ruled India from the 16th
century. Versions of it differ
all over the subcontinent, and
there is lively debate over how
(or if) it differs from *pulao*,
or *pilaf*. The key differences:
biryani is layered, with stronger
spices, and plays the starring
role of the meal.

INDIA

HYDERABADI CHICKEN BIRYANI

SERVES 6

A bowl fit for an emperor – rice infused with precious spices, and meat simmered in yoghurt – simplified here for the modern table, but retaining all its comforting deliciousness.

METHOD

1 Wash the rice, soak it for 30 minutes and drain for 30 minutes.

2 Cut the chicken thighs in half along the bone; the pieces will be unevenly sized with the bone in one half. Rub with salt and pepper.

3 Heat the oil in a large frying pan and fry the onion, garlic and ginger until onion is golden. Add the chilli, cumin, tomatoes and a pinch of salt and pepper. Stir-fry for 5 minutes. Add the yoghurt, cardamom and cinnamon.

4 Cover and cook over a low heat, stirring occasionally until the tomatoes are pulpy (adding a little hot water if necessary).

5 When the mixture is thick and smooth, add the chicken and stir to coat. Cover and cook over very low heat until the chicken is tender and the sauce has reduced, 30–40 minutes.

6 For the rice, heat the oil in a large casserole and fry the onions until golden. Add the cardamom, cloves, cinnamon and ginger and stir. Add the rice and stir to coat with spices.

7 Heat the stock separately and pour it over the rice. Add the saffron water. Stir and let simmer for 8 minutes, until rice is half cooked.

8 Stir and add the chicken mixture, mixing it into the rice. Cover, turn heat to very low and steam for 10–15 minutes without lifting the lid.

9 Spoon into deep bowls, scatter coriander and fried onions on top and serve with *dahi* or yoghurt on the side.

TASTING NOTES

On the subcontinent, *biryani* is a phenomenon, with countless restaurants specialising in this cult dish. It's an essential feature of Muslim wedding feasts, and households guard their family recipes, perfected over generations. Made in the traditional way, this is no 15-minute budget buster – it was prepared for banquets, often over several days, and its saffron content made it a dish for the rich. Real-deal Hyderabadi *biryani* is made using the *dum* method – the meat and rice are placed in a pot sealed with *chapati* dough to keep the steam in and the flavours vivid. Our version is simpler but no less delicious – for an extra hit of authenticity serve with *dahi* chutney (yoghurt, mint and onion) and *baghara baingan* (roasted eggplant). ● *by Janine Eberle*

ORIGINS

The word jambalaya is said to combine the French word for ham (*jambon*) with *à la* (meaning 'with') and *ya*, a West African word for rice, though this may be apocryphal. Born in Cajun Country Louisiana, it was probably an attempt to make paella without saffron. Local cooks substituted tomatoes for colour and flavour, and the dish became popular among frugal home cooks looking to make a hearty meal with whatever odds and ends were in the house.

LOUISIANA, USA

JAMBALAYA

SERVES 6

**Iconic enough to inspire a classic country song (Hank Williams'
'Jambalaya (On the Bayou)'), jambalaya is the original fusion cuisine,
a rice and meat concoction with a thousand possible variations.**

YOU'LL NEED
2 tsp olive oil
2 boneless chicken breasts,
   chopped into 2.5cm (1in)
   pieces
260g (9oz) Andouille sausage,
   sliced
1 onion, peeled and diced
1 capsicum (bell pepper),
   diced
1 celery stick, diced
2 garlic cloves, peeled and
   chopped
½–1 tsp cayenne pepper
½ tsp onion powder
salt and pepper, to taste
400g (14oz) white rice
4 cups chicken stock
3 bay leaves
2 tsp Worcestershire sauce
1 tsp hot sauce (such as
   Tabasco)

METHOD
1 In a large pan, heat the oil over medium-high heat. Saute the chicken and Andouille sausage until lightly browned.

2 Add the onion, capsicum, celery, garlic, cayenne, onion powder and salt and pepper.

3 Cook, stirring, until the onions are soft and translucent, about 5 minutes.

4 Add the rice, chicken stock and bay leaves. Bring to the boil, then reduce the heat, cover and simmer for 20 minutes.

5 Stir in the Worcestershire sauce and hot sauce and serve.

TASTING NOTES
Jambalaya is best known as a home-cooked dish, a staple of family Sunday lunches or church picnics. And everyone's *grandmère* makes the best version, *mais oui*! Non-natives can seek jambalaya at the more casual – some might say divey – pubs and late-night haunts of New Orleans. Order a steaming bowl of whatever's on special that night – gamey rabbit, salty-savoury sausage, sweet crayfish – and chow down, shaking more vinegary Louisiana hot sauce on to taste. Each bite holds dozens of flavours – the freshness of rice, the meaty chew of Andouille, the sting of garlic, the brininess of shrimp. Cool your sizzling taste buds with a chilled Abita ale, brewed just 30 miles away at NOLA. ● *by Emily Matchar*

YOU'LL NEED
370g (13oz) dried egg noodles
vegetable oil

For the curry paste
5cm (2in) piece of fresh
    ginger, peeled and chopped
    into large pieces
5 large garlic cloves, peeled
2–3 red chillies
1 medium onion, peeled and
    roughly chopped

For the curry
vegetable oil
1 tsp turmeric powder
1kg (2lb 2oz) skinless and
    boneless chicken thighs, cut
    into 2.5cm (1in) pieces
salt
800ml (1⅓ pints) coconut milk
1 tbs chickpea (besan) flour

For the toppings
bunch of fresh coriander
    (cilantro) leaves and stems,
    roughly chopped
1 cup chopped spring onions
    (scallions)
1 red onion, peeled and very
    thinly sliced
4 hard-boiled eggs, cut into
    wedges
4 lemons, cut into wedges
chilli powder, gently roasted in
    a pan or oven

ORIGINS

Khow suey (pronounced cow-
swè) comes from the Burmese
term for noodles, *hkuauq-swèh*.
The dish originated in Burma's
Shan State, a mountainous
region bordering China to
the north, Laos to the east
and Thailand to the south, so
variations of the dish can also be
found in the markets of northern
Thailand and Laos. The recipe
for *khow suey* also travelled to
Eastern India with Indians who
fled Burma during World War II,
so it's often served among the
Indian community.

SERVES 4

MYANMAR (BURMA)

KHOW SUEY

This fragrant Burmese noodle dish is a riot of flavours
and textures that can be served as a 'build your own
bowl' crowd-pleaser, perfect for entertaining.

METHOD

1 To make the curry paste, grind the ginger, garlic, red chillies and onion into a thick paste in a mortar and pestle or food processor.

2 Heat 2 tbsp of oil in a heavy-based pan and add the curry paste and turmeric. Heat gently, stirring, until fragrant.

3 Add the chicken, season with salt and cook until tender, 10–15 minutes

4 Add half of the coconut milk and simmer gently for 10 minutes.

5 Stir the chickpea flour through the remaining coconut milk and add to the pan, warming through on a low heat.

6 Cook the egg noodles in a pan of boiling water and drain.

7 Heat 1½ cups of vegetable oil a small pan until very hot (about 5 minutes). Taking 2 cups of the cooked noodles, fry about ½ cup at a time, spreading them out thinly with a fork to ensure they cook through.

8 When golden, remove with a slotted spoon, drain on paper towels and break into smaller pieces for serving.

9 To serve, place the boiled noodles in a bowl and spoon over the chicken curry. Top with coriander, spring onions, red onion, hard-boiled egg wedges and fried noodles. Squeeze over lemon juice and a sprinkle of roasted chilli powder.

TASTING NOTES

Slurp up the silky egg noodles coated in creamy coconut curry and savour the freshness of the coriander (cilantro), spring onions (scallions) and ginger. Enjoy the crispy texture and audible crunch of the fried noodles then wait for the roasted chilli powder to deliver its earthy kick. Be sure to squeeze a generous amount of lemon juice over your bowl to add another taste element and make every ingredient sing. Party time? *Khow suey* is ideal for entertaining large groups – line up the noodles, curry and assorted toppings and invite your guests to 'build your own bowl', tailor-making their dish to their own palate. ● *by Alison Ridgway*

ORIGINS

Kuaytiaw is yet another Chinese contribution to Thailand's street food repertoire. Originally introduced by Chinese labourers, who popularised the dish during the early 20th century, today *kuaytiaw* is hands down the most common street food in Thailand. Versions involving spices and a curry-like broth were probably introduced via Muslim traders, while more recent spin-offs have resulted in a vast repertoire of entirely Thai varieties.

SERVES 1

THAILAND

KUAYTIAW

Kuaytiaw, or Thai noodle soup with pork or fishballs,
is – dare we say it – the hamburger of Thai street food:
it's simple, satisfying, cheap and ubiquitous.

YOU'LL NEED
1¼ cups pork or chicken stock
50g (2oz) fresh rice noodles
  or 40g (1½oz) dried rice
  stick noodles
5 small pork balls or 2 tbs
  shredded cooked chicken
1 tsp ground white pepper
handful of beanshoots,
  trimmed
handful of coriander (cilantro)
  leaves, chopped
fried garlic or onion flakes
spring onions (scallions),
  chopped
red chillies, chopped
wedge of lime

METHOD
1 Boil the stock in a small pan.

2 Add the noodles, pork balls or chicken and white pepper and simmer for a few minutes, until the noodles are cooked.

3 Pour the soup into a bowl and top with the beanshoots and coriander leaves.

4 Garnish with the fried garlic or onion flakes, spring onions and as much chilli as you can handle. Squeeze over some lime juice. Serve immediately.

TASTING NOTES
Kuaytiaw is Thai comfort food, and doesn't pack the spicy punch of most of its counterparts. Yet despite its apparent simplicity, ordering *kuaytiaw* the Thai way requires a bit of knowledge, as diners are expected to specify what type of noodles they want, as well as their preference for meats or other toppings. Like other Thai noodle-based dishes, *kuaytiaw* comes out of the kitchen relatively bland and customers then season it with optional condiments including fish sauce, sugar, dried chilli flakes and vinegar. *Kuaytiaw* vendors span the most diverse spectrum of Thai street eats, and range from gritty streetside stalls to air-conditioned restaurants. Likewise, the dish functions equally well as breakfast, a late-night snack and anything in between. ● *by Austin Bush*

YOU'LL NEED

For the tomato sauce

3 tbs olive oil
½ cup finely chopped onion
4 garlic cloves, peeled and
    chopped
400g (14oz) passata
¾ tsp ground cinnamon
½ tsp ground cumin
½ tsp salt
¼ tsp ground black pepper
¼ tsp chilli flakes

For the kushari

1 cup long grain rice
1 cup lentils (brown or black)
2 tbs white vinegar
½ tsp ground cumin
½ tsp garlic powder
8 tbs olive oil
1½ cups sliced onion
1 cup pasta (small macaroni or
    vermicelli broken into small
    pieces)

ORIGINS

This cheap, filling and healthy
national dish is so popular that
some restaurants specialise in
this alone, but little is known
about its genesis. Educated
conjecture suggests that it
may have been created out
of poverty or that, as vegan
victuals, it was influenced by
the vegetarian diet of fasting
Coptic Christians. Whatever
the case, meat – such as small
pieces of fried liver, chicken or
lamb – is now sometimes back
in the bowl.

EGYPT

KUSHARI

SERVES 8

Opinions often diverge in Egypt, but one thing almost every Egyptian concedes is that *kushari* – a unique medley of pasta, rice and lentils with tomato sauce – reigns supreme.

METHOD

For the tomato sauce

1 Heat the oil and onions on a medium flame until the latter are golden brown.

2 Stir in the garlic and cook for 2 minutes.

3 Add the passata, cinnamon, cumin, salt, pepper and chilli flakes. Increase the heat a bit and let simmer, uncovered, until the sauce thickens (approximately 15–20 minutes).

For the kushari

1 Simultaneously, but in different pans, cook the rice and the lentils. The lentils should simmer, covered, until tender (20–30 minutes); then, use a strainer to remove the lentils (leaving the lentil water in the pot), placing them directly into a mixture of the vinegar, cumin and garlic powder.

2 Heat the oil on a medium flame; add the onions and cook, deglazing as necessary, until they are lightly browned. Remove from the oil and drain on paper towel.

3 Stir the uncooked pasta into the same oil used for cooking the onions; saute the pasta until it is lightly browned, then place it in the used lentil water, bring back to a boil and cook until tender.

4 Assemble the *kushari* in eight bowls: lay down a base of rice, add a blanket of pasta with a few browned onions, and then a covering of lentils.

5 Spoon the tomato sauce on top and garnish with a few more onions.

TASTING NOTES

Kushari is a delectable, any-time-of-day, year-round whole that is more addictive than the sum of its humdrum parts: pasta, rice and lentils. The magic finish comes from a spicy tomato-sauce topping and garnish of fried onions, all enhanced by garlic-vinegar or chilli. It is assembled in a few seconds – but the experience is downright percussive. In *kushari*-specific restaurants, the cooked ingredients are doled out from a drum set of food-filled basins. As it happens, the *kushari* composer raps his spoon against the bowls and basins in a virtuoso display of rhythm. It's loud but mesmerising, a *Stomp*-style performance that begs an encore. Or is it just that the *kushari*'s so good one bowl is never enough? ● *by Ethan Gelber*

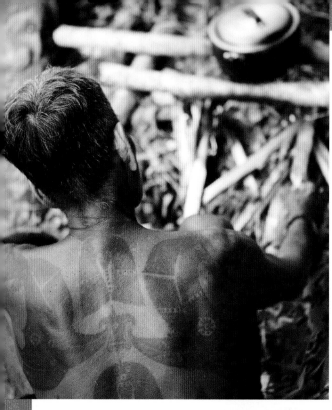

YOU'LL NEED
8 cups water
Sarawak *laksa* paste
8 prawns (shrimp)
2–3 cups chicken stock
½ cup coconut milk
2–3 eggs
butter, for frying
2 handfuls of *bee hoon*
  noodles
1 handful of beanshoots
110g (4oz) shredded cooked
  chicken breast
coriander (cilantro) leaves,
  to garnish
1 lime
sambal belacan, to taste

ORIGINS

Most purveyors of Sarawak *laksa*
are, like *bee hoon* noodles,
of Chinese origin, but in the
finest Malaysian tradition this
dish brings together a variety
of culinary influences, including
classic Nyonya (Peranakan)
ingredients like *sambal belacan*.
Sarawak *laksa* shares little more
than its name with the *laksa*
dishes of Peninsular (West)
Malaysia and Singapore, such as
asam laksa (fish and tamarind
soup) and curry *laksa* (a fusion
of curry and coconut milk).

SARAWAK, MALAYSIA

SARAWAK LAKSA

SERVES 2

Tangy, spicy, oh-so slurpable and lip-smackingly good, Sarawak *laksa* is a supremely satisfying way to begin the day. It's the dish Sarawakians most often crave when they're away from Borneo.

METHOD

1 In a pan, bring the water to the boil then add the Sarawak *laksa* paste. Stir every few minutes for 30–45 minutes.

2 In a separate pan, boil the prawns in the chicken stock until cooked, then remove and slice lengthwise.

3 Add the chicken stock to the Sarawak *laksa* pan. Simmer over a low heat for a few minutes.

4 Pour the liquid into a third pan through a fine-mesh strainer to remove any solid particles. Continue to simmer.

5 Add coconut milk to taste. Stir the broth every few minutes.

6 Beat the eggs, the fry in a little butter to produce a very thin omelette; slice into strips.

7 Soak the *bee hoon* noodles in hot water until soft, then place in boiling water for 3 minutes. Transfer the noodles to two medium-sized bowls.

8 Add the beanshoots, shredded chicken breast, halved prawns and omelette strips to the bowls.

9 Ladle just enough broth into the bowls to cover the noodles.

10 Garnish with chopped coriander leaves and squeeze the juice of half a lime into each bowl.

11 Add *sambal belacan* to taste.

TASTING NOTES

You're in Kuching and it's 7.30am, so following a tip you stroll to a cafe famous for its Sarawak *laksa*. Inside, men and women – mostly Chinese, but also Malay and Dayak – read newspapers or chat in a babel of dialects as they dig into oversize bowls with chopsticks and spoons. Inside each one, a tangle of vermicelli noodles, swimming in oil-flecked broth, is topped with crunchy beanshoots, orange-white shrimp, strips of omelette, chicken bits and vibrant coriander leaves. Occasionally, someone adds a dollop of fiery *sambal belacan* or a squeeze of calamansi lime. The air is redolent with the tang of chilli, galangal and lemongrass and the heady aromas of coriander and coconut milk. ● *by Daniel Robinson*

YOU'LL NEED

200g (7oz) macaroni
2 tbs butter, plus extra
   for greasing
1½ tbs plain (all-purpose)
   flour
1½ cups milk
grating of nutmeg
½ tsp mustard powder
50g (2oz) mature (sharp)
   Cheddar
salt and pepper
⅓ cup coarse breadcrumbs
1 tbs grated parmesan

ORIGINS

Baked dishes of pasta and cheese have been recorded as far back as the 14th century, including a recipe for 'makerouns' in the medieval English cookbook *Forme of Cury* – a simple lasagne-style concoction of fresh pasta, grated cheese and butter. It hasn't changed much since. The story goes that Thomas Jefferson established its popularity in the USA after sampling it in Europe, but it was Kraft's boxed mac 'n' cheese, introduced in 1937, that secured its place as a fast-food icon.

SERVES 2

USA

MACARONI AND CHEESE

Is there a more perfect comfort food than mac 'n' cheese? Its appeal lies in its simplicity – it's a bland beige hug of a bowl recommended for hangovers, rainy days and bed-bound binge-watching.

METHOD

1 Cook the macaroni in plenty of salted boiling water until tender. Drain and rinse under cold running water.

2 Meanwhile, melt two-thirds of the butter in a pan and stir in the flour. Cook, stirring, for a couple of minutes, then take off the heat and gradually whisk in the milk (using a whisk) until you have a smooth sauce. Cook, stirring, for a few minutes until it thickens, then add the nutmeg and mustard powder. Stir in the Cheddar until smooth and season to taste.

3 Pre-heat the grill. Grease a baking dish with butter, then combine the pasta and cheese sauce and tip it into the dish.

4 Melt the remaining butter and toss it with the breadcrumbs and parmesan. Spread over the top of the dish, then grill for about 10 minutes until golden and bubbling.

TASTING NOTES

From its humble beginnings, mac 'n' cheese has attained a level of stardom rare for bowls of pasta, with online forums, festivals and whole restaurants devoted to it. The big question – stovetop versus baked – stirs passions; in her standard-setting Victorian *Book of Household Management*, the famous Mrs Beeton plumps for stovetop with a final baking stage (as we have done here). Debate also rages over acceptable additions: nutmeg? (we think so), eggs? (probably unnecessary), garlic? (definitely not). If you were to visit one of many mac 'n' cheese restaurants found stateside, you'd have more options – lobster, truffle and jalapeños (not in the same bowl) are popular additions. But we say keep it simple – a sharp cheese, plenty of butter, and crunchy breadcrumbs grilled on top to offset the uncomplicated gooey richness.

● *by Janine Eberle*

ORIGINS

The earliest written record of *manti* can be found in an Ottoman cookbook from the 15th century, but the original recipe travelled down the Silk Road from Central Asia and is considered an ancient offshoot of the Chinese dumplings we know today. *Manti* in Anatolia is a general term applied to tiny stuffed and boiled wheat pockets, usually served with a generous dollop of garlic yoghurt on top.

YOU'LL NEED

For the dough
4 cups flour (more for dusting)
1 tsp coarse salt
3 eggs, lightly beaten
1 cup cold water

For the filling
125g (4½oz) ground lamb
125g (4½oz) ground beef
3 medium onions, peeled and grated
2 tbs clarified butter
1 bunch fresh parsley, finely chopped
1 tsp coarse salt
1 tsp ground pepper

For cooking
12 cups low-sodium beef or chicken stock
salt
450g (1lb) plain Greek yoghurt
4 garlic cloves, peeled, minced and mashed to a paste
230g (8oz) unsalted butter
3 tsp dried mint
1 tsp *urfa biber* (Turkish red pepper) or paprika

TASTING NOTES

Long ago, it was said that a desirable bride should be able to make her *manti* in such a delicate fashion that 40 dumplings could fit in the palm of her husband's hand. And that's still a rule to work by when perfecting the dumplings in the modern Turkish kitchen. This recipe comes from famed Turkish cookbook writer and lecturer Nevin Halici. She notes that 'each of the tiny dumplings should be the size of your fingertip, easily serving 25 to 30 per person,' and continues by suggesting that the making of *manti* is just as important as its consumption. 'It's traditional to invite two or three friends to help fill and seal the *manti*; after all, many hands make light work.' ● *by Brandon Presser*

TURKEY

MANTI

**Anatolia's comfort food, the dumpling-like shape of *manti*
is a strong reminder that Turkey is the ultimate melting pot,
evolving ancient recipes from Central Asia and beyond.**

SERVES 10

METHOD

1 To make the dough, combine all ingredients in a large bowl, gradually adding the water to form a smooth mass.

2 On a lightly floured surface, knead for 5–8 minutes, until smooth.

3 Form the dough into two balls, cover with a damp towel and leave to rest for 1 hour.

4 To make the filling, gently combine all of the ingredients in a large bowl.

5 Roll out the dough on a lightly floured surface until 4mm thick, then cut into 3cm (1¼in) squares.

6 Spoon ¼ tsp of the filling into the centre of each square.

7 Gently stretch the opposite corners of each square outwards then bring them together and pinch to seal. Repeat with the other two corners. Repeat with all the squares.

8 Place the completed dumplings on a baking sheet lightly dusted with flour and cover with a damp towel.

9 Bring the stock to a boil in a large pan.

Gently simmer the *manti* until tender and cooked through, around 5 minutes.

10 Stir together the salt, yoghurt and crushed garlic in a bowl. Add about ¼ cup of the stock and stir well.

11 Slowly melt the butter until amber.

12 Use a slotted spoon to transfer the *manti* to individual bowls.

13 Top the *manti* with some garlic-yoghurt sauce, a drizzle of browned butter, and sprinkle with mint and pepper or paprika.

YOU'LL NEED

50g (2oz) rice
1 tbs vegetable or canola oil
1 onion, peeled and finely
    diced
1 tsp fresh ginger, peeled and
    crushed
1 tsp turmeric
2 tbs shrimp paste
2 red chillies, chopped
50g (2oz) banana stem, sliced
    thinly
2 lemongrass stalks, sliced
    thinly
3 cups fish stock
50g (2oz) gram flour
450g (1lb) dried thin rice
    noodles
200g (7oz) firm white fish,
    such as haddock, pollack or
    sea bass, sliced
lime wedges, fried onions,
    extra chopped chillies and
    fresh coriander (cilantro)
    leaves, to serve

ORIGINS

Mohinga is made from an almost
exclusively indigenous repertoire
of ingredients, suggesting
that the dish has its origins in
Myanmar. Some suspect that
the noodles, which are made
from rice by a complicated and
time-consuming process that
is thought to date back several
centuries, are also indigenous
to the region. This stands
in contrast with most other
Southeast Asian noodle dishes,
which can usually be traced
directly back to China.

SERVES 4

MYANMAR (BURMA)

MOHINGA

Cherished as Myanmar's national dish, *mohinga* is a comforting noodle soup that exemplifies the earthy flavours of the country's cuisine via a combination of lemongrass, shallots, turmeric and freshwater fish.

METHOD

1 To prepare the rice, toss it in a heated pan until the grains are browned and slightly burned (but not stuck to the pan) and crush using a mortar and pestle or a spice grinder. (Alternatively, the amount of gram flour can be doubled in place of the toasted rice.)

2 Heat the oil in a pan and fry the onion, ginger, turmeric, shrimp paste, chillies, banana stem and lemongrass until the onion has softened – about 15 minutes.

3 Add the stock and whisk in the gram flour and toasted rice. Simmer for approximately 15 minutes, until the soup has thickened.

4 Add the rice noodles and continue simmering until the noodles are cooked.

5 Add the fish and cook for a further 5 minutes, until the fish is opaque and cooked through.

6 Serve immediately with a wedge of lime and garnished with fried onions, chopped chillies and coriander leaves.

TIP *Banana stems look like fibrous white leeks and taste very similar to the fruit. If you're unable to find them in Asian grocery stores, try substituting water chestnuts.*

TASTING NOTES

Generally associated with central Myanmar and that region's predominantly Burmese ethnic group, *mohinga* is nonetheless sold in just about every town in Myanmar, typically from mobile vending carts and baskets or basic open-fronted restaurants. *Mohinga* vendors are most prevalent in the morning. Ordering the dish is a simple affair, as the only optional ingredient is *akyaw* (crispy fritters of lentils or battered and deep-fried vegetables). The thick broth has flakes of freshwater fish (typically snakehead fish), a yellow/orange hue due to the addition of turmeric, and a light herbal flavour, thanks to the use of lemongrass. A bowl is generally seasoned in advance, but dried chilli and limes are usually available to add a bit of spice and tartness. ● *by Austin Bush*

ORIGINS

Also known as Indonesia's national dish, *nasi goreng* sprang from humble beginnings. Originally a trick to avoid wasting rice, it was served as breakfast the next day, mixed with leftover scraps of chicken or beef and fortified with shrimp paste and *kecap manis* (Indonesia's answer to soy sauce). It's most likely that the dish originated with Chinese fried rice – trade between the two countries began around the 10th century – although a competing theory goes that it was inspired by Middle Eastern *pilaf*, brought by Arabic traders.

INDONESIA

NASI GORENG

Born from the need to use up yesterday's leftover rice, this traditional Indonesian breakfast, powered by shrimp paste and sweet soy sauce, is a crowd-pleaser for any meal.

YOU'LL NEED

2 tbs peanut or vegetable oil
1 tsp dried shrimp paste
2 medium shallots, peeled and thinly sliced
2 garlic cloves, peeled and thinly sliced
1 tsp finely sliced red chilli or *sambal oelek*
4 cups cold cooked long grain rice
1 tbs *kecap manis* (sweet soy sauce)
salt, to taste
2 eggs
2 spring onions (scallions), thinly sliced
½ cucumber, sliced, to serve
prawn crackers, to serve (optional)

METHOD

1 Heat 1 tbs oil in a wok on a low heat. Add the shrimp paste and cook until brown and aromatic.

2 Add the shallots and garlic and stir-fry until fragrant and golden brown.

3 Add the chilli followed by the rice. Turn up heat to moderate and stir-fry until all the rice is warm and the ingredients are well mixed. Sprinkle the rice with water if necessary to keep it moist.

4 Add the *kecap manis* and stir until evenly distributed. Season with salt to taste.

5 Heat the remaining oil in another pan and fry the eggs sunny side up.

6 Sprinkle the rice with sliced spring onions and serve in bowls, topped with a fried egg, with a few slices of cucumber and prawn crackers on the side.

TASTING NOTES

Across Indonesia, you'll find *nasi goreng* being touted by cart-pushing hawkers, sizzling in *warung* (street food stall) woks and on the menu at the finest restaurants, as well as on every family table. Ask for 'special' to get a fried egg on top; ask for it *'pedas'* and you're playing with fire – diced fresh chilli will be thrown into the wok while it's cooking. The variations are endless. *Nasi goreng ayam* comes with spicy fried chicken; *nasi goreng ikan bilis*, popular in Flores, Komodo-dragon territory, contains small dried anchovies. *Nasi goreng gila*, or 'crazy fried rice', rarely found outside Jakarta, might contain sausage, scrambled egg, meatballs, chicken gizzards and whatever else the chef feels like throwing in – even corned beef. That's the beauty of *nasi goreng* – anything goes. ● *by Janine Eberle*

YOU'LL NEED

1 cup short grain white rice
4 eggs
2 cups *dashi* (or chicken stock)
4 tbs soy sauce
1 tbs sugar
200g (7oz) chicken thighs,
   skinned, boned and
   chopped into bite-sized
   pieces
2 spring onions (scallions),
   finely sliced

ORIGINS

The original Japanese fast
food, *donburi* emerged as a
'convenience food' during the
Meiji period of the late 19th
and early 20th century – the
era of railways, steamships and
industry – as lifestyles became
faster-paced and the need
emerged for a nourishing lunch
or snack to eat on the run. The
popularity of *donburi* endures
today as a versatile and practical
meal option, as well as being a
tasty way to repurpose leftover
rice and other dishes.

SERVES 2

JAPAN

OYAKO DONBURI

This hearty meal of chicken and eggs with rice, whose name literally means 'parent and child', is a comforting and beloved staple of Japanese cuisine.

METHOD

1 Cook the rice according to the packet instructions. Set aside and keep warm.

2 Mix the eggs in a bowl, being careful not to overbeat, then set aside.

3 In a medium frying pan, combine the *dashi*, soy sauce and sugar and bring to a boil.

4 Reduce the heat slightly and add the chicken. Simmer for about 10 minutes or until the chicken is cooked.

5 Gently pour in the eggs in a steady stream in and around the chicken. Do not stir.

6 Let the egg start to set, being careful not to overcook, before stirring once (the egg will finish cooking on contact with the hot rice). Remove from the heat.

7 To serve, put some rice in each bowl and top with the chicken and egg mixture. Garnish with spring onion.

TASTING NOTES

Visit any Japanese restaurant around the world and you're bound to come across a *donburi* dish, easily recognisable on the menu as 'don', such as *tendon* (tempura on rice) or *katsudon* (pork cutlet on rice). To make *donburi*, hot rice is topped with all manner of meat, fish, egg or vegetables, garnished with pickles and gently doused in a *dashi*-based sauce. Often served in a specially made deep-footed bowl about double the size of a small rice or miso soup bowl and eaten with chopsticks, *donburi* is a culinary staple in Japan, commonly eaten at home and found everywhere from railway stations to speciality restaurants serving only this single bowl-based hero dish. ● *by Johanna Ashby*

ORIGINS

Phat thai, which allegedly dates back to the 1930s, is a relatively recent introduction to the Thai kitchen and, despite the nationalistic name, is in many ways more of a Chinese than a Thai dish. Both noodles and the technique of frying are Chinese in origin, although the dish was invented in Thailand and its seasonings are characteristically Thai. Today, it is quite possibly Thailand's most beloved culinary export and remains a popular one-dish meal in Bangkok and central Thailand.

YOU'LL NEED

4 tbs tamarind concentrate
6 tbs palm sugar
2 tbs fish sauce
5 tbs peanut (groundnut) or vegetable oil
8 red shallots, peeled and coarsely chopped
3 duck eggs
320g (11oz) fresh rice noodles; or 260g (9oz) dried rice noodles, blanched in boiling water
50g (2oz) firm tofu, cut into cubes
2 tbs dried prawns (shrimp), rinsed and dried
1 tsp salted radish, rinsed, dried and finely chopped
2 tbs roasted peanuts, coarsely chopped
2 handfuls of beanshoots, trimmed
1 handful of Chinese chives, sliced into 2.5cm (1in) lengths
extra beanshoots and roasted peanuts, fresh chillies and lime wedges, to serve

SERVES 4

THAILAND

PHAT THAI

Phat thai is the most famous Thai dish in the world, and understandably so: you can't go wrong with gooey strands of noodles, crunchy peanuts, tart lime and singed egg.

METHOD

1 Mix the tamarind concentrate with the palm sugar and fish sauce until the sugar dissolves. Set aside.

2 Heat the oil in a wok over medium heat.

3 Fry the shallots until they begin to colour.

4 Crack in the eggs and stir them until they resemble scrambled eggs.

5 Turn up the heat and add the blanched noodles. Add the tamarind mixture and let it simmer for a few minutes.

6 Stir in the tofu, dried prawns, radish and peanuts and continue stirring until most of the sauce is absorbed.

7 Add the beanshoots and chives and stir for a few minutes.

8 Transfer to a bowl, top with more beanshoots and roasted peanuts and serve immediately with fresh chillies and lime wedges on the side.

TIPS _Have all the ingredients prepared and ready to go next to your wok as the dish takes very little time to cook._

The duck eggs may be substituted with chicken eggs, and the red shallots with French shallots or brown onions but the rest of the ingredients are key to the dish's salty, sweet and sour taste, and should be readily available from Asian supermarkets.

TASTING NOTES

Although nowadays _phat thai_ is sold in restaurants, it's still an important part of the street-food repertoire. Stalls selling the noodles also tend to serve _hoy thot_, a mussel omelette. Both are generally fried on the same flat, round surface, but some vendors choose to fry _phat thai_ in a wok. _Phat thai_ is among the milder Thai street dishes and diners are expected to boost the flavour with a personalised mixture of fish sauce, sugar, dried chilli and ground peanuts. Served with sides that possess a slightly bitter taste, including banana flower and garlic chives, true _phat thai_ is a largely vegetarian dish containing only dried shrimp and fish sauce, although modern versions sometimes include fresh prawns or shrimp.

● _by Austin Bush_

ORIGINS

Pho has its origins in the cuisines of France and China and was popularised around the end of the 19th century. The Vietnamese took the rice noodles from their northern neighbour and a taste for red meat from the colonialists, and created something new. Some say *pho* (pronounced 'feu') is derived from the French dish *pot au feu*, while others argue that it is Chinese in origin, stemming from a Cantonese word for noodles, *fan*.

YOU'LL NEED

For the broth

10cm (4in) piece of ginger root
2 yellow onions
cooking oil
2.25kg (5lb) beef marrow or oxtail bones
4.75L (5 quarts) of water
1 cinnamon stick
1 tsp coriander seeds
1 tbs fennel seeds
5 star anise
2 cardamom pods
6 whole garlic cloves
¼ cup fish sauce
2 tbs sugar
1 tbs salt

For the noodles & garnishes

230g (8oz) beef steak
450g (1lb) dried flat rice noodles
10 sprigs of mint
10 sprigs of coriander (cilantro) leaves
10 sprigs of Thai basil
12 sawtooth coriander leaves
½ yellow onion, peeled and thinly sliced
2 limes, each cut into 6 thin wedges
2–3 chillies, sliced
450g (1lb) beanshoots
hoisin sauce
hot chilli sauce

TASTING NOTES

Dawn is breaking across Vietnam and the hum of scooter engines has yet to reach its mid-morning crescendo. The *pho* sellers have set up stalls, some little more than a battered collection of metal pans, while others include plastic tables and gleaming trolleys. Whatever you choose, it's the broth that matters. This is the heart and soul of *pho* and should be rich and deeply flavoured, hinting at star anise, cardamom and coriander. The noodles should be freshly made, while the chillies are mild, rather than fierce. Beanshoots add a satisfyingly crunchy texture. A dash of fish sauce, a squeeze of lime, and breakfast is ready. Grab a wobbly chair, sit back and slurp. ● *by Tom Parker Bowles*

SERVES 8

VIETNAM

PHO

The breakfast of champions, this fragrant spiced Vietnamese noodle soup topped with slices of beef, brisket, chicken or meatballs and a squeeze of lime is the perfect wake-up call.

METHOD

For the broth

1 Halve the ginger and onions lengthwise and place on a baking sheet.

2 Brush with cooking oil and put on the highest rack under a heated grill (broiler). Grill on high until they begin to char. Turn over to char the other side for a total of 10–15 minutes.

3 Boil enough water in a large pan to cover the beef bones and continue to boil on high for 5 minutes.

4 Drain, rinse the bones and rinse out the pan. Refill the pan with the bones and the 4.75L (5 quarts) of cool water. Bring to the boil then lower to a simmer. Remove any scum that rises to the top.

5 Place the cinnamon stick, coriander seeds, fennel seeds, star anise, cardamom pods and garlic cloves in a mesh bag (alternatively, *pho* spice packets are available at speciality Asian food markets) and add to the broth pan along with the charred onion and ginger and the fish sauce, sugar and salt. Simmer for 1½ hours.

6 Discard the spice pack and the onion and continue to simmer for another 1½ hours.

7 Strain the broth and return it to the pan. Adjust salt, fish sauce and sugar to taste.

For the noodles & garnishes

1 Slice the beef steak as thinly as possible across the grain.

2 Cook the noodles according to the packet instructions, until tender.

3 Bring the broth back to the boil.

4 Arrange all the other garnishes next to your serving bowls.

5 To serve, fill each bowl with noodles and raw meat slices. Ladle the boiling broth into the bowls – this will cook the beef slices.

6 Garnish with the remaining herbs, onion, lime wedges, chillies, beanshoots and sauces, and serve immediately.

YOU'LL NEED

4½ cups chicken stock
900g (2lb) green peas in the pod, podded, pods reserved
40g (1½oz) butter
1 onion, peeled and finely chopped
200g (7oz) pancetta, cut into batons
½ cup chopped flat leaf parsley
1½ cups risotto rice, preferably *Vialone Nano*
½ cup grated parmesan, plus extra, to serve
salt and pepper, to taste

ORIGINS

This dish's impressive pedigree dates to the Venetian Republic, when it was prepared on 25 April to celebrate the feast day of the city's patron saint, Mark, and served with much ceremony to the Doge. This tradition marked the appearance of the first peas to the Rialto market, and thus the arrival of spring. Purists insist on using peas from Chioggia, at the southern entrance to the lagoon of Venice, and *Vialone Nano* rice grown on the Veronese plains.

SERVES 4

VENICE, ITALY

RISI E BISI

This celebrated Venetian dish traditionally uses locally grown rice and fresh peas – and not much else. It's a soothing, salty-sweet bowl perfect for midweek meals – just don't ask whether it's soup or risotto.

METHOD

1 Warm the chicken stock in a stockpot and add the rinsed pea pods. Simmer for 10–15 minutes to allow pea flavour to infuse.

2 Heat half the butter in a large saucepan. Add the onion and pancetta and cook until the onion starts to colour, about 10 minutes.

3 Add the peas, half the parsley and a ladle of hot stock. Bring to the boil then add the rice. Stir well.

4 Add the rest of the broth and cook over medium-low heat, stirring gently from time to time to stop it sticking.

5 When the rice is al dente, stir in the parmesan and remaining butter and parsley, then season to taste with sea salt and freshly ground black pepper. Divide among four bowls and serve immediately, with extra parmesan on the side.

TASTING NOTES

It can be a challenge to eat well in Venice. Our tip: avoid the tourist restaurants filling the *piazzi* and seek out backstreet *bacari* (wine bars). Often small and unassuming, these casual, usually cheap spots are where you'll find local dishes done well, eaten alongside real-life Venetians. Just don't get into an argument over the perfect consistency of *risi e bisi* – it's a question on which even the experts are divided. Is it a soup, requiring a spoon to eat, or a fork-necessitating risotto? Let the last word be *all'onda*, 'like a wave', the consistency benchmark for northern Italian rice dishes. Either way, the saltiness of pancetta against the bursts of chlorophyll sweetness from fresh peas, held in balance by creamy, buttery rice, is a humble revelation. ● *by Janine Eberle*

SERVES 6

ORIGINS

Singapore noodles' history is
elusive, but it definitely is *not*
from Singapore. A common
belief is that Cantonese
chefs invented it to reflect
multicultural influences. Given
its popularity in countries like
the UK and the USA, a more
likely beginning involves Western
chefs attempting to replicate
the fusion flavours of Singapore-
style noodles, such as *char kway
teow* (from China) and *mee
goreng* (Indian/Malay origins).

YOU'LL NEED

320g (11oz) dried rice noodles
2 tsp Madras (hot) curry
  powder
1 tsp ground turmeric
3 tbs light soy sauce
2 tbs rice wine or sherry
½ cup chicken stock or water
vegetable oil, for stir-frying
3 medium eggs, beaten
140g (5oz) medium raw
  prawns (shrimp)
100g (3½oz) chicken breast,
  sliced into strips
1 garlic clove, peeled and
  crushed
2cm (¾in) piece of ginger,
  grated
1 medium red chilli, chopped
4 spring onions (scallions),
  chopped
1 small green capsicum, sliced
  thinly
100g (3½oz) *char siu* pork,
  sliced thinly
140g (5oz) bean sprouts
chopped spring onions
  (scallions) and coriander
  (cilantro), to garnish
lime wedges, to serve

CHINA (HONG KONG), UK, USA, CANADA,
AUSTRALIA (EVERYWHERE BUT SINGAPORE!)

SINGAPORE NOODLES

A tantalising blend of subtle curry and oriental flavours
and a surf-and-turf combination of pork and prawns make
Singapore noodles a winning fusion of East and West.

METHOD

1 Soak the noodles in boiling water for a few minutes until soft, then drain the water and set aside.

2 Make the sauce by combining the curry powder, turmeric, soy sauce, rice wine or sherry and chicken stock in a small bowl.

3 Put 1 tsp oil in a wok on medium-high heat, scramble the eggs, then take them out of the wok and set aside.

4 Add a little more oil. Sear, but do not cook, the prawns and set aside.

5 Add a little more oil if necessary, cook the chicken and set aside.

6 Put 1 tbs oil in the wok, then quickly fry the garlic, ginger, chilli and spring onions for a few minutes.

7 Add the sauce and the capsicum and heat until the sauce is simmering.

8 Toss in the noodles, stirring to coat, then return the prawns, chicken and egg to the wok and add the pork and bean sprouts. Stir-fry for a few minutes.

9 Garnish with the spring onions and coriander. Serve immediately with lime wedges.

TIP *Have all your ingredients prepared and ready to go in the wok for fast cooking. Feel free to use more or less chilli according to taste.*

TASTING NOTES

A complete meal in itself, nothing beats Singapore noodles when you have a craving for a savoury, protein-laden, moreish treat. The dish is an explosion of flavours and textures – smoky curry provides plenty of oomph to soft chicken and tender prawns (shrimp), balanced by the sweet *char siu* and crispy vegetables. Golden-hued noodles, green capsicum and deep-red pork also make for a veritable feast for the eyes. This cheap and filling dish is found everywhere from street food stalls to teahouses, restaurants and everything in between, not to mention being a cinch to cook at home. Variations include the addition of cabbage, mushrooms or sesame oil. ● *by Johanna Ashby*

ORIGINS

Meaty sauces date back to Roman times, but it was the Gauls who transformed the recipe into something similar to what we know today. These early *ragù* dishes were tomato-free – that would come with the arrival of tomatoes in Europe from the New World in the 16th century. As for the pasta, serving *ragù* with spaghetti (made from durum wheat and originating in Naples) is unheard of in the hometown of 'spag bol', where it's served with wide, flat tagliatelle made from fresh eggs.

TASTING NOTES

Here in Bologna – '*la Grassa*' (the Fat One) – beats Italy's gastronomic heart. The immense popularity of its most famous dish has led to infinite variations so, in a bid to establish first principles, in 1982 the Bolognese chamber of commerce set down an official recipe (our recipe here hews closely to it). While it may surprise some (no tomatoes! milk?) it's more like what you'll find in a Bolognese kitchen than in the world's red-sauce restaurants – an *umami* bomb of meatiness, concentrated by long, slow cooking and transported perfectly by silky smooth egg pasta. To try it at its best, get yourself invited to the home of a local *nonna*. If that fails, choose a traditional *trattoria* and make sure you ask for *tagliatelle al ragù* – not spaghetti Bolognese. ● *by Janine Eberle*

SERVES 2

BOLOGNA, ITALY

TAGLIATELLE AL RAGÙ

When you go to Bologna, where the dish known and loved as 'spaghetti Bolognese' was invented, you'll find a slightly different manifestation of what may be the world's favourite bowl of comfort.

YOU'LL NEED

1 tbs butter
140g (5oz) pancetta, cut into small cubes
2 celery sticks, finely chopped
1 small carrot, peeled and finely chopped
½ small onion, peeled and finely chopped
300g (10½oz) ground beef
½ cup dry white wine
5 tsp tomato paste
1 cup whole milk
salt and pepper, to taste
fresh egg tagliatelle
shaved parmesan cheese, to serve

METHOD

1 Melt the butter in a pan and add the pancetta. Cook gently until the fat has rendered, about 10 minutes.

2 Add the celery, carrot and onion and cook, stirring frequently, until soft and lightly browned, about 15 minutes.

3 Add the ground beef and cook while stirring, until lightly browned and starting to sizzle.

4 Add wine and cook until evaporated, about 5 minutes.

5 Mix the tomato paste with a little water and add to the pan.

6 Reduce the heat to low and simmer for 2 hours, stirring occasionally, adding the milk little by little and adjusting the seasoning.

7 Bring some salted water to a boil in a large pan and cook the tagliatelle until al dente.

8 Toss the pasta with the *ragù* and serve with the parmesan.

ORIGINS

Once the speciality of one restaurant in Jinan, the capital of Shandong Province, this stew became a staple of the royal palace kitchen in the 16th century when Emperor Jiajing was presented with the dish in Beijing, and immediately loved it. News of his approval spread among nobility, celebrities and literati in Jinan, making the dish famous in the province. Centuries later, there has been a recent spike in its popularity, with restaurants specialising in yellow braised chicken rice popping up all over modern-day China.

SERVES 2

JINAN, CHINA

YELLOW BRAISED CHICKEN RICE

Soybean paste adds *umami* richness to this stew of tender chicken, shiitake mushrooms and green peppers, which is being rediscovered centuries after it first captivated an emperor.

YOU'LL NEED

2 boneless chicken thighs, skin on
vegetable oil
1 tsp raw sugar
2 tbs Shaoxing (Chinese cooking) wine
1cm (½in) piece fresh ginger, finely sliced
5 small red chillies, chopped
2 tbs yellow soybean paste
4 dried shiitake mushrooms, soaked in water, sliced
2 green capsicums, cut into 2cm (¾in) pieces
1 tsp white pepper
½ tsp salt
steamed rice, to serve

METHOD

1 Chop the chicken into 4cm (1½in) pieces.

2 In a pan, add a splash of oil and the sugar. Heat slowly to melt and gradually brown the sugar, stirring constantly.

3 Add the chicken, increase the heat and stir quickly. Stir in the cooking wine, ginger, chilli and yellow soybean paste.

4 Pour in water to cover the chicken. Add the mushrooms, capsicums, white pepper and salt.

5 Cover to stew on a low heat for 15–20 minutes, until the chicken is tender, but the soup is not too thick.

6 Spoon into deep bowls, with small side bowls of steamed rice to mix in at the table.

TASTING NOTES

The restaurant is alive with the tinkle of clay pots, ceramic bowls and teacups. The one-bowl nature of this dish means you'll find plenty of solo diners immersed, silent, in their feast. When you lift the lid on your bowl, the chicken should glisten a deep golden brown, in small tender pieces that fall away from the bone. The rich, fermented soybean broth is a perfect match with the chicken and juicy shiitake; the green bell pepper provides texture. Take the accompanying bowl of rice and mix it all in, letting it smooth out the saltiness of the broth and provide a comforting carbohydrate platform. ● *by Phillip Tang*

STEWS, BRAISES & HEARTY BOWLS

Most of the world's cuisines have their big bowls of meaty comfort. These are often the relics of traditional peasant food, many of them thrifty ways to stretch the household budget or make the most of the whole beast. A fragrant pot of *boeuf bourguignon* or spicy South African *bredie* simmering away on the stovetop can banish the greyness of a winter day. And if meat's not your thing, dig into hearty meat-free classics such as Indian *dal* and Moroccan red bean *tajine*.

🥣 Easy   🥣 🥣 Medium   🥣 🥣 🥣 Hard

ORIGINS

Technically meatballs, *bakso* are almost always associated with their eponymous soup, which is sold by street vendors around Indonesia. The name originates from the Hokkien word for shredded meat so the dish is likely of Chinese-Indonesian origin. Today, *bakso* has travelled all over Southeast Asia to be mixed into myriad tasty broths from Vietnam to Singapore. No matter what regional ingredients are added, the dish always keeps the three basics: meatballs, noodles and broth.

YOU'LL NEED

For the meatballs

3 tbs peeled diced shallot
vegetable oil, for frying
450g (1lb) ground beef or chicken
3 tbs tapioca starch
1 egg white
1 tbs sugar
salt and pepper

For the broth

3 garlic cloves, crushed
1 tbs fresh ginger, grated
½ tsp vegetable oil
1.8L (1½qt) beef/chicken stock
1 stick celery
1 tsp sugar
1 tsp pepper
1 tsp lime juice
1 tsp fish sauce
salt, to taste
400g (14oz) egg or rice
   noodles, cooked al dente

Optional garnishes

1 bunch of bok choi, blanched
spring onion, chopped
fried shallots
boiled eggs
sambal (chilli sauce), to taste

SERVES 6

JAVA, INDONESIA

BAKSO

Subtly seasoned broth and tasty meatballs are the culinary equivalent of a warm hug. Take a break from regional, fiery spices to enjoy Indonesia's most humble yet well-loved street food.

METHOD

For the meatballs

1 Fry the shallots in the vegetable oil in a small pan over medium heat until golden.

2 Transfer to a food processor and add the meat, tapioca starch, egg white, sugar and seasoning and process until very well ground. Place the paste in a bowl and refrigerate, covered, for at least 2 hours.

3 Put a pan of water on to boil. While waiting, form the meat paste into balls about 2½cm (1in) in diameter.

4 Drop the meatballs into the boiling water. Once each ball floats to the surface of the water, cook them an additional 2 minutes. Set aside.

For the broth

1 Lightly saute the garlic and ginger in the oil in a small frying pan, until fragrant.

2 Add to a large pan with the stock and celery and simmer for several minutes.

3 Remove the celery stick and add the remaining ingredients.

4 Ladle into individual bowls and add meatballs to each. Garnish as desired.

TASTING NOTES

Portable *bakso* stalls, with their aluminium pan for broth and a shelf or two for meatballs, noodles, vegetables and other fixings, are often pedalled around by bicycle from late afternoon through the night in Indonesia, from the smallest country town to exhaust-filled Jakarta. With its savoury, not-spicy broth, slippery noodles and gently seasoned meatballs, *bakso* is perfect sustenance for a stop on a long, curvy bus ride, a late night on the town or nourishment after a bout of tummy trouble. ● *by Celeste Brash*

ORIGINS

Once a peasant staple, *bigos* is now Poland's national dish. Since the 17th century, cookery books have described it as a hash or bake of fish, meat and various leftovers. The recipe was perfected as a hearty cabbage stew and became embedded in Poland's consciousness when 19th-century writer Adam Mickiewicz devoted 20 lines to praising *bigos* in *Pan Tadeusz*, the country's national epic. In modern Poland, *bigos* bubbles away for Easter and Christmas. Ingredients vary, but every Pole swears by mum's own recipe.

YOU'LL NEED

1 large green cabbage, shredded
3 tbs vegetable oil
1 onion, peeled and roughly chopped
200g (7oz) bacon, roughly chopped
260g (9oz) mushrooms, quartered
3 garlic cloves, peeled and crushed
4 cups vegetable or chicken stock
400g (14oz) canned tomatoes
200g (7oz) sauerkraut
3 tbs tomato paste
1 tsp juniper berries
½ tsp black peppercorns
3 bay leaves
¼ cup dried mushrooms
1 tsp smoked paprika
4–5 *kabanosy* (sticks of smoked, dried Polish sausage)

SERVES 4

POLAND

BIGOS

The smoky aroma of *bigos* is enough to make any Pole yearn for grandma's home cooking. This nutritious stew is infused with juniper, forest mushrooms and a dash of Polish history.

METHOD

1 Blanch the shredded cabbage in a pan of boiling water for about 4 minutes, then drain and set aside.

2 Heat the oil in a large pan over medium heat. Add the onion, bacon and mushrooms, stirring for a couple of minutes.

3 Add the garlic while stirring, and cook for another minute.

4 Reduce the heat to low and pour in the stock and canned tomatoes.

5 Add the blanched cabbage, sauerkraut, tomato paste, juniper berries, black

peppercorns, bay leaves, dried mushrooms and smoked paprika. Stir thoroughly.

6 Chop the *kabanosy* into 4cm- (1½in-) long pieces and stir them in.

7 Turn the heat as low as possible and cover the pan, or transfer the mixture to a slow-cooker, if you have one.

8 Leave to simmer for around 7 hours, stirring every couple of hours. It's ready to eat in 3 hours if you can't wait any longer.

TASTING NOTES

Good *bigos* can't be rushed. It's slow-cooked for hours, sometimes days, to bring its flavours to fullness. Poles swear that it's tastiest when reheated the next day, which gave rise to its nickname of 'hunter's stew': a delicious meal for a lone hunter to reheat over an open fire. In Polish homes, the family's nostrils are tickled by the aroma of smoky sausage and pungent cabbage stewing for days before the *bigos* is finally served. But what a pay-off: a slurpable stew stained reddish with spices and dense with cabbage; the luckier spoonfuls containing a hunk of *kabanos*, chewy dried sausage. There's no thickener used in *bigos*, so a hunk of rye bread is ideal for mopping up the juices. ● *by Anita Isalska*

SERVES 4

YOU'LL NEED

1 tbs olive oil
200g (7oz) unsmoked bacon,
    cut into 2½cm (1in) batons
1.5kg (3½lb) stewing beef
    (cheek, chuck or shin), cut
    into 5cm (2in) pieces
2 tbs plain (all-purpose) flour
1 onion, peeled and finely
    chopped
1 carrot, peeled and finely
    sliced
3 garlic cloves, peeled and
    minced
1 bottle Burgundy or another
    good-quality light red wine
1½ tbs tomato paste
bouquet garni
2-3 cups beef stock
3 tbs butter
340g (12oz) pearl onions or
    shallots, peeled
340g (12oz) small button
    mushrooms
salt and pepper, to taste
boiled potatoes, crusty bread
    or potato puree, to serve

ORIGINS

The dish we know today is the
work of two famous chefs, one
French, one American. Auguste
Escoffier, the great moderniser
of French cuisine, published
his recipe in 1903; Julia Child,
in *Mastering the Art of French
Cooking*, updated it for the
home cook in 1961. But you
can tell it's a peasant cuisine
classic by its long, slow cooking
time and the local provenance
of its traditional ingredients –
Charolais cattle from southern
Burgundy and the region's
celebrated Pinot noir wine.

FRANCE

BOEUF BOURGUIGNON

Sure, it's sophisticated bowl food, but don't be intimidated by this French classic. It's not hard to make, and will fill your home with the heavenly smell of beef slowly braising in red wine. Comfort food par excellence.

METHOD

1 Melt 1 tbs olive oil in a heavy casserole over medium-high heat. Add the bacon and fry until golden, then scoop out with a slotted spoon and set aside.

2 Roll the beef in flour, and in the same pan, fry in batches, without overcrowding, until deeply browned. Set aside.

3 In the same pan, cook the chopped onion, carrot and garlic over medium heat for 3-4 minutes, until softened, stirring frequently. Add the wine, tomato paste and bouquet garni. Bring to a boil, scraping the bottom of the pan.

4 Return the beef and bacon to the pan with enough stock to cover. Cover the pan and simmer gently, stirring occasionally, until the meat is very tender (about 3 hours).

5 While the meat is cooking, heat 1 tbs butter in a large frying pan, add the pearl onions or shallots and saute over medium heat for about 10 minutes, rolling to brown evenly. Set aside

6 Heat 2 tbs butter in the same pan, add the mushrooms and toss for 5 minutes, until lightly browned.

7 Add the onions and mushrooms to the pan with the meat after 2½ hours of cooking. Season to taste and cook, covered, for 30 minutes more.

8 Serve with boiled potatoes or crusty bread, or boost the comfort factor with a buttery potato puree.

TASTING NOTES

Not far from the centre of France, Burgundy (Bourgogne in French) likes to claim it's the country's gastronomic heart. You'll find around 30 Michelin-starred restaurants in the region, but for a traditional, non-deconstructed *boeuf bourguignon* hunt down a classic bistro such as Ma Cuisine in Beaune. It's the stuff that French dining dreams are made of – stumbling across an unassuming little *resto* in a hidden alleyway and receiving a warm welcome into a cosy, modest dining room. Leaving a couple of hours later, replete after an earthy *terrine de campagne*, a bowl of rich *boeuf bourguignon*, slow-braised for hours in good local wine and perhaps some pungent *époisses de Bourgogne* cheese to finish. *Bon appétit!* ● by Janine Eberle

ORIGINS

A 'bunny', as the locals call their bread-loaf meals, has several rumoured origins, all rooted in Durban's Indian community. Does it date back as far as the 1800s, as a way for Indian indentured labourers to transport their meals to the plantations? Did it start as an ingenious packed lunch for Indian golf caddies? Or did it develop during the early years of apartheid, when, with black clients prohibited from eating in restaurants, local Indian chefs served them portable curries from their restaurants' kitchens and side doors?

YOU'LL NEED

1 tsp cumin seeds
1 tsp fennel seeds
1 cinnamon stick
1 star anise
4 green cardamom pods
2 tbs vegetable oil
1 onion, peeled and finely chopped
1 tbs fresh ginger, minced
1 tbs minced garlic
2 tbs *garam masala*
1 tsp ground coriander
2 tsp turmeric
1 tsp cayenne pepper
1kg (2lb 2oz) lamb or beef, diced
4 tomatoes, chopped
8 curry leaves
1¼ cups vegetable stock
2 large potatoes, chopped into bite-sized pieces
2 tbs chopped coriander (cilantro)
juice of 1 lemon
2 loaves crusty white bread, cut in half and hollowed (soft insides reserved)

SERVES 4

SOUTH AFRICA

BUNNY CHOW

**Durban's favourite takeaway is a thick, spicy curry
of meat or beans complete with its own edible
bowl – a hollowed-out loaf of white bread.**

METHOD

1 Fry the cumin seeds, fennel seeds, cinnamon stick, star anise and cardamom pods in the oil until they start to sizzle.

2 Add the onion and cook for 15 minutes, or until translucent.

3 Add the ginger, garlic, *garam masala*, ground coriander, turmeric and cayenne pepper and fry for 1 minute, then add the meat and stir to mix.

4 Add the tomatoes, curry leaves and stock. Bring to the boil, then reduce the heat and simmer, stirring occasionally, for 1 hour or until the meat is tender.

5 Add the potatoes and ¾ cup water. Continue simmering until the potatoes are cooked (10–15 minutes).

6 Stir in the chopped coriander and lemon juice.

7 To serve, spoon into bread bowls. Use the loaf's fluffy insides to mop up the curry.

TASTING NOTES

The sultry seaside city of Durban is the best place to sample a bunny, and come lunchtime, curry joints and takeaway kiosks across the metropolis throng with a mix of office workers, labourers and hipsters. Whether made with chicken, lamb or traditional sugar beans, your bunny should be rich and gently spiced, with a lump of the loaf's soft insides (known as the 'virgin') balanced on the top, and fiery pickles and sambal on the side. There's no better way of attack than digging in with your hands, demolishing the curry-soaked bread bowl as you go along. Managing to eat without making a mess takes practice, however – rip too enthusiastically and you'll send the saucy contents tumbling across your plate. ● *by Nana Luckham*

ORIGINS

First baked in sun-kissed Languedoc, *cassoulet* began as a thrifty use of leftover meat with a beany base. The wide-rimmed *cassole* in which it's cooked allows a thick crust to form, and gave this epic stew its name. Castelnaudary claims to have first invented the dish, Carcassonne's local *cassoulet* includes a medley of mutton and partridge, but Toulouse's recipe is arguably the finest. It makes use of the region's two culinary heroes: melt-in-the-mouth duck and chubby, garlic-infused *saucisses de Toulouse*.

YOU'LL NEED

1 tbs olive oil
1 garlic bulb
½ cup duck fat
2 duck legs
4–6 coarse pork sausages, ideally *saucisses de Toulouse*
1 small onion, peeled and finely diced
2–3 carrots, peeled and finely diced
800g (1¾lb) tinned haricot beans
4 bay leaves
1 sprig of thyme
½ tsp sea salt
2 cups chicken stock
¾ cup wholemeal breadcrumbs
crusty bread, to serve

TOULOUSE, FRANCE

CASSOULET

SERVES 4

**Both nourishing and naughty, this steamy bake combines
haricots, *saucisse de Toulouse* (garlicky local sausage)
and decadent duck that practically falls off the bone.**

METHOD

1 Preheat oven to 180°C (350°F). Rub olive oil on the garlic and wrap it in foil, then place it in the oven for 30 minutes.

2 Heat half the duck fat in a pan, and fry the duck legs for 4 minutes on each side, until golden. Set aside.

3 In the same fat, fry the sausages until slightly browned (about 12 minutes). Set aside.

4 Gently fry the onions and carrots in the fat for 15 minutes or until cooked through, then transfer into a casserole dish (ideally a *cassole*, with a rim wider than its base).

5 Halve the sausages and slice pieces from the duck legs. Put it all (including the bones) into the dish.

6 Carefully unwrap the garlic and use a spoon to squish roasted garlic from each clove.

7 Add the beans, roasted garlic, bay leaves, thyme and salt to the dish. Add enough stock to cover all the ingredients and stir well.

8 Cover the cassoulet and place in the oven for 1½ hours.

9 Add remaining duck fat to a clean pan. Fry breadcrumbs for 1 minute, stirring briskly.

10 Stir the cassoulet, sprinkle on the fried breadcrumbs, and return to the oven (without a lid) for another 30 minutes.

11 Serve in deep bowls with crusty bread on the side.

TASTING NOTES

Appropriately for a slow-cooked recipe, the flavours of a cassoulet unfold gradually. First, there's the fragrant steam, redolent with unholy amounts of roasted garlic. You break through the breadcrumb crust to reveal still-juicy sausage and spears of meltingly tender duck meat hiding among almost caramelised beans. From the first loaded forkful, it's clear the haricots are no mere filler: they act as a vehicle for all the fatty notes of the sausage and duck, each bite carrying deep, smoky flavours. It's well worth fork-jousting for the half-sausages hiding under the crust – a sparring match best suited to one of Toulouse's vaulted cellar restaurants. ● *by Anita Isalska*

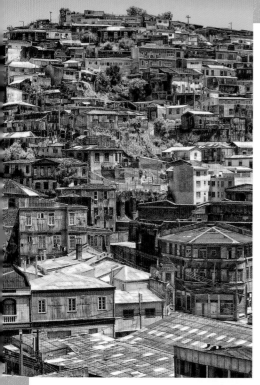

ORIGINS

Charquicán is derived from '*charquikanka*', a Quechua/ Mapuche word meaning 'stew with jerky'. For hundreds of years, the people of the Andes preserved their meat (often llama) by drying and salting it. Treasured by travelling merchants, peasants and soldiers, it was served in hearty soups, accompanied by regional vegetables. As time passed, however, llama meat – and the strong taste of any jerky – fell out of favour, to be replaced by fresh ground or shredded beef.

CHILE

CHARQUICÁN

Llama jerky is no longer the choicest meat for this vegetable-rich Andean stew. Still, young Latinos often crave *charquicán* as a favourite flavour of their youth.

YOU'LL NEED

2 tbs olive oil
230g (½lb) ground or shredded beef, cubed *chicharrón* or shredded chicken
1 medium onion, peeled and diced
¼ tsp dried oregano
½ tsp ground cumin
salt and pepper, to taste
6 medium potatoes, peeled and cubed
230g (½lb) pumpkin (squash), peeled and cubed
1 garlic clove, minced
1 cup *choclo* (large-kernel corn) kernels
½ cup , chopped green beans
4 eggs

METHOD

1 In a large heavy-bottomed pan, heat the olive oil over medium-high heat. Add the meat and saute for 4 minutes.

2 Add the onion and cook for 4 more minutes.

3 Sprinkle on the oregano, cumin, and salt and pepper to taste. Stir for 1 minute.

4 Add potatoes, pumpkin, garlic and 2 cups water. Cover partly and let simmer until potatoes are soft (15–20 minutes).

5 Lightly mash the potatoes and pumpkin.

6 Mix in the *choclo* and green beans and cook for 5 minutes.

7 In a separate pan, fry the eggs (one for each person) sunny side up.

8 Serve the *charquicán* in four bowls, each topped with an egg.

TASTING NOTES

Charquicán is a favourite family feast in both winter and summer. These days, it's the mix of vegetables that most influences its flavour, texture and nutrition. Potatoes add starchy heft, while pumpkin (squash) contributes its natural sweetness, as do corn and optional touches such as green beans or peas. The taste is enhanced by onion, garlic, herbs and spices. Throughout the Andean region, there are many variations of traditional *charquicán*, both in ingredients and in preparation. For instance, it can be made with chicken or no meat at all, and sometimes with seaweed as a protein substitute. In the Argentine and modern Chilean versions, a fried egg is perched on top. ● *by Ethan Gelber*

YOU'LL NEED

6–8 dried whole chillies
  (pasilla, guajillo, New Mexico,
  or a mixture)
1½ tsp ground cumin
½ tsp ground black pepper
salt
2¼ cups water
5 tbs lard
1kg (2lb 2oz) of well-trimmed
  and cubed (1½cm/½in) beef
  chuck
⅓ cup finely chopped peeled
  yellow onion
3 cloves of garlic, minced
2 cups beef stock
2 tbs *masa harina* (corn flour)
1 tbs muscovado brown sugar,
  firmly packed
1½ tbs white vinegar
sour cream, to serve
lime wedges, to serve

ORIGINS

Stories of chilli's origin are as varied and fantastical as versions of the recipe today. One Native American legend credits 17th-century Spanish nun Sister Mary of Agreda (though she never set foot in America), while another theory suggests immigrants from the Canary Islands introduced the dish. Most likely, however, is that it was created for cattle drivers – dried beef, fat, chillies and salt pounded into bricks that could be rehydrated while traversing between Texas and California.

TEXAS, USA

CHILLI CON CARNE

SERVES 4

This behemoth of bowl foods, laden with beef and chillies,
is much like a hug from your mother – its rich embrace
dispels your ills and whispers 'all will be well'.

METHOD

1 Gently toast the chillies in a large frying pan over medium-low heat for 2–3 minutes. Place in a bowl, cover with boiling water and soak until soft, 30–45 minutes. Drain and split, then remove seeds and stems.

2 Thoroughly blend the chillies with the cumin, black pepper, 1 tbs salt and ¼ of the cup water to create a smooth, fluid paste. Set aside.

3 Melt 2 tbs lard in the frying pan over medium-high heat. When it starts to smoke, add the beef in batches and cook for 6 minutes or until lightly browned. Set aside.

4 Melt the remaining lard and add the onion and garlic. Cook gently, stirring occasionally, for 3–4 minutes, then pour in the stock and remaining 2 cups of water.

5 Whisk in the *masa harina* gradually, then stir in the chilli paste. Add the beef with its juices and turn up the heat.

6 Once the mixture starts to simmer, reduce the heat to a low simmer. Cook for 2 hours, stirring occasionally, until the meat is tender.

7 Thoroughly stir in the muscovado sugar and vinegar and season to taste. Gently simmer for another 10 minutes. Remove from the heat and let stand for at least 30 minutes.

8 If the chilli seems too dry, add more stock or water; simmer more if it's too wet. Add more salt, sugar, or vinegar to taste.

9 Reheat gently and serve in bowls with sour cream and lime wedges.

TASTING NOTES

Depending on your tolerance for spices, a spoonful of chilli con carne can generate a variety of responses, from wrapping your palate in a figurative fuzzy blanket to blasting it with a blowtorch. And therein lies the joy of making your own: you can establish your perfect level of heat. Chillies aside, the flavours in the bowl are always warming, with garlic, onions, beef and a variety of spices each playing their part. In Texas (where it is the official state dish), it's just known as 'chili' or 'bowl o' red', and in purist's recipes you won't find beans, tomatoes or minced beef (steak or brisket is used). ● *by Matt Phillips*

YOU'LL NEED
8 medium potatoes
5 tbs butter
230g (8oz) Savoy cabbage or
  curly kale, shredded
12 spring onions (scallions),
  finely chopped
⅓ cup single cream
ground nutmeg
salt and pepper, to taste

ORIGINS

Using easily available, year-round ingredients, colcannon was cheap and simple to cook, making it a staple in Irish homes for centuries, often served with boiled ham. It is celebrated in song, and a key part of Halloween traditions when a ring, a thimble and coins added to the mix predict an impending marriage, a life alone or untold wealth. In some parts of Ireland, unmarried women tied a sock filled with colcannon to the front door – the first man to enter would be their future husband.

SERVES 4

IRELAND

COLCANNON

Smooth, comforting and creamy colcannon is a humble variation on mashed potato and, when served with a melting knob of salty butter, the quintessential taste of home for many Irish people.

METHOD

1 Boil the whole potatoes for 20 minutes or until tender.

2 Heat 2 tbs of the butter in a large pan and lightly fry the cabbage or kale for 3 minutes.

3 Add the spring onions and cook for another minute.

4 Drain the potatoes, peel off the skins, then mash until smooth.

5 Add the cream, nutmeg, 2 tbs of the butter and mix well. Season to taste with salt and pepper.

6 Serve in large bowls, making a well in the centre for the remaining knob of butter.

TASTING NOTES

Imagine sitting in your mother's kitchen as an Irish child, barely old enough to see over the top of the stove, the smell of boiling potatoes and melting butter wafting through the air, your only care in the world that you get served dinner before your greedy brothers. Somehow, colcannon brings back that deep-seated sense of contentment and expectation with its smooth texture and the golden well of melted butter glistening at its heart. Sinking your spoon into the creamy mixture, dipping into the butter and letting it glide into your mouth was quite simply the pinnacle of a happy childhood in country Ireland. ● *by Etain O'Carroll*

ORIGINS

Deriving its name from the Sanskrit for 'to split', *dal* is a food as ancient as Indian culture itself. Archaeological evidence points to its first appearance in the Bronze Age during the Indus Valley Civilization (3300–1300 BC), where lentils were a staple ingredient. Early Indian texts even contain *dal* recipes used to impress guests. A *dal* revival occurred in medieval India (8–18th centuries AD), when slow cooking in steam gained popularity. There's been no stopping it ever since.

YOU'LL NEED

3 tbs oil (or 2¼ tbs ghee or butter)

1 large onion, peeled and chopped

1–2 green chillies, chopped

2cm (¾in) fresh ginger, peeled and finely chopped

2 tsp turmeric

1 cup split lentils (yellow or red, or ½ cup of each), rinsed

2 bay leaves

1 cinnamon stick

½ tsp *garam marsala*

2 tbs chopped coriander (cilantro) leaves

salt, to taste

1 tsp cumin seeds

2 garlic cloves, peeled and crushed

2–3 dry red chillies

½ tsp red chilli powder

2 tbs lemon juice

steamed rice, Indian bread or papadum, to serve

INDIA

DAL TADKA

Colourful and zesty, this South Asian lentil stew is as ubiquitous, multipurpose and beloved on the Indian subcontinent (and beyond) as mashed potatoes in middle America.

METHOD

1 In a large pan, cook 1 tbs olive oil (or ¾ tbs ghee or butter) over medium-high heat. Add the onion, green chillies, ginger and turmeric, and saute for 2 minutes.

2 Add the rinsed lentils, bay leaves, cinnamon and water to cover. Bring the water to a boil, then cover, reduce the heat and simmer, stirring occasionally, until the lentils are creamy and soft (30–35 minutes).

3 Add the *garam masala*, 1 tbs of the coriander and salt to taste. Mix and set aside.

4 Heat 2 tbs oil (1½ tbs ghee or butter) in a frying pan. Over low heat, add the cumin seeds and fry until fragrant, then add the red chillies and garlic. Stir until the garlic is browned, then add the red chilli powder. Stir in the lemon juice and remove from the heat.

5 Pour the contents of frying pan into the *dal*. Mix or don't mix – both approaches are fine.

6 Garnish with the remaining chopped coriander and serve hot with steamed rice, Indian bread or papadum.

TASTING NOTES

Though it seems humble, *dal* is arguably the one dish to which all Indians, regardless of origin, class or caste, have a strong connection. Yellow split lentils are the most common *dal* ingredient worldwide, but Indian *dals* – and even more so *dals* across South Asia – come in a dazzling range of textures, colours, flavours and piquancy, based on local culinary traditions and the many varieties of spices and split pulses (lentils, peas and beans) that serve as the main ingredients. Eaten as a main course, *dal* is usually accompanied by rice or breads like *roti, chapati* and *naan*, but it is just as often one of several dishes composing a more complex meal, like most Indian *thalis*. ● *by Ethan Gelber*

ORIGINS

Said to have been a favourite of Jonathan Swift, the author of *Gulliver's Travels*, and mentioned in the works of Joyce, coddle is a very Dublin dish. It was the busy housewife's ally, quick to prepare, easy on the household budget and happy to be left simmering endlessly until 'himself' stumbled in from the pub. Traditionally, it was cooked on a Thursday night to use up any leftover sausages and bacon before Friday, a fast day for Irish Catholics when meat was avoided.

DUBLIN, IRELAND

DUBLIN CODDLE

SERVES 4

A slow-cooked dish of sausage, bacon and potato, coddle
is a one-pot wonder far greater than the sum of its parts.
On a cold winter night, it's comfort food at its finest.

YOU'LL NEED

285g (10oz) good-quality pork
sausages
200g (7oz) dry-cured bacon
2 medium onions, peeled and
roughly chopped
4 large carrots, peeled and
roughly chopped
3 tbs chopped parsley
salt and pepper
¾ cup stock
8 medium potatoes, peeled
and quartered
Irish soda bread, to serve

METHOD

1 Lightly grill the sausages and bacon until slightly coloured.

2 Preheat the oven to 180°C (350°F).

3 Arrange the onions and carrots in the bottom of a large
oven-proof dish.

4 Scatter with half the parsley, season with salt and pepper
and add the stock.

5 Arrange the sausages on top of the vegetables, then the
potatoes and bacon in layers above them.

6 Scatter with more parsley and season.

7 Cover and cook in the oven for 1 hour.

8 Remove the lid and return to the over for another 30 minutes.

9 Serve with crumbly Irish soda bread to soak up the juices.

TASTING NOTES

A bowl of coddle feels like a warm embrace on a cold winter's evening when the drizzle has
left you soaked through and the heat of the fire just can't take the chill away. It's the kind of
dish that tastes best after ages spent gently simmering on a cast-iron range, clothes airing
on slats above the cooker, a kettle simmering and a cat curled up on an armchair. Although
it's a very forgiving dish that can be left for hours on end with little more than a splash of
extra water to nourish it, a good coddle depends largely on the quality of the meat – so
don't scrimp when buying your ingredients. ● *by Etain O'Carroll*

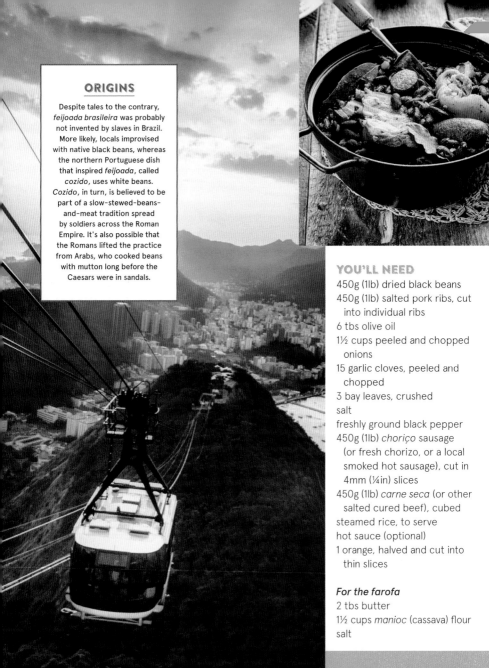

ORIGINS

Despite tales to the contrary, *feijoada brasileira* was probably not invented by slaves in Brazil. More likely, locals improvised with native black beans, whereas the northern Portuguese dish that inspired *feijoada*, called *cozido*, uses white beans. *Cozido*, in turn, is believed to be part of a slow-stewed-beans-and-meat tradition spread by soldiers across the Roman Empire. It's also possible that the Romans lifted the practice from Arabs, who cooked beans with mutton long before the Caesars were in sandals.

YOU'LL NEED

450g (1lb) dried black beans
450g (1lb) salted pork ribs, cut into individual ribs
6 tbs olive oil
1½ cups peeled and chopped onions
15 garlic cloves, peeled and chopped
3 bay leaves, crushed
salt
freshly ground black pepper
450g (1lb) *choriço* sausage (or fresh chorizo, or a local smoked hot sausage), cut in 4mm (¼in) slices
450g (1lb) *carne seca* (or other salted cured beef), cubed
steamed rice, to serve
hot sauce (optional)
1 orange, halved and cut into thin slices

For the farofa

2 tbs butter
1½ cups *manioc* (cassava) flour
salt

BRAZIL

FEIJOADA

SERVES 4

Think soul food, Brazilian style: a stick-to-the-ribs, flavourful (but not spicy), purplish stew of beans (*feijão* in Portuguese) and salted or smoked meat that always begs for *mais, por favor*.

METHOD

1 Soak the beans overnight in cold water. Separately soak the ribs.

2 Drain beans, then cover with cold water. Bring to a boil over medium heat and simmer for 30 minutes. Stir occasionally, skim foam and add water if necessary to keep beans covered.

3 Over medium heat, warm 4 tbs of the olive oil in a large, heavy-bottomed pan, then add the onions and 6 cloves of chopped garlic and cook until softened.

4 Add the bay leaves, season with salt and pepper, and saute for 5 minutes.

5 Add the *choriço* or other sausage and cook for 5 minutes.

6 Add the cubed beef, ribs (and optional meats) and beans with the cooking liquid. Mash about one-eighth of the beans to release starch.

7 Bring to a boil, reduce the heat and simmer until the beans are tender and the meat falls off the bone (1½–2½ hours). Add water to keep the beans covered and ensure the stew is rich, not gluey. Season to taste.

8 In a separate saute pan, make the *farofa*. Melt the butter over a medium heat. Add the *manioc* flour and season with salt. Saute until golden (3–5 minutes).

9 Serve the *feijoada* over steamed rice. Sprinkle on hot sauce if desired and garnish with *farofa* and orange slices.

TASTING NOTES

Feijoada isn't eaten quickly. Leisurely appreciation is demanded by the rich and hefty mix of simmer-softened beans, tender pork (trimmings, bacon, ribs, sausage) and jerked beef, all topped with toasted manioc flour (*farofa*) and served with rice, sauteed collard greens and palate-cleansing oranges. It is perfectly suited to a long and slow weekend feast with family, friends and something worth celebrating. Although claimed by Brazilians as their national dish, *feijoada* is hardly uniform. In fact, it is as satisfying, vibrant and diverse as Brazil's people and culture. The choice of meats differs cook by cook, for example, and red or brown kidney beans are common in parts of the country, as is a heavier emphasis on vegetables. ● *by Ethan Gelber*

YOU'LL NEED

2 tbs oil

1 tsp fenugreek seeds

3 sprigs of curry leaves

3 garlic cloves, peeled and
  finely chopped

2 onions, peeled and thinly
  sliced

6–8 small pickled red chillies,
  diced

3 tbs Madras curry powder

2 cups water

2 tbs tamarind paste

salt, to taste

1 large (about 1kg/2lb 2oz) red
  snapper head

8 large okra, cut lengthwise

230g (½lb) fried tofu, cubed

2 big tomatoes, cut into
  quarters

1 cup coconut milk

1 tbs chopped fresh coriander
  (cilantro) leaves

ORIGINS

As with many Peranakan dishes,
the roots of fish head curry
can be traced back to the early
days of nautical migration and
trade between East Asia, South
Asia and the West. While today's
dish might seem, at first glance,
more heavily influenced by its
South rather than East Asian
roots, the Chinese fondness for
fish head is well known, making
the Peranakan version – like
Singapore itself – a shining
example of cultural cooperation.

SERVES 4

SINGAPORE & MALAYSIA

FISH HEAD CURRY

Though most Westerners shy away from dishes in which the main ingredient's eyes are included, Singaporeans swear it's the fish's head that contains the sweetest meat in this soupy curry.

METHOD

1 Heat the oil in a large soup pan over a medium heat, add the fenugreek seeds and saute for 1 minute.

2 Add the curry leaves and garlic and saute for another minute.

3 Add the onions and chillies and fry for about 10 minutes, until the onions are light brown.

4 Add the curry powder and fry for another 5 minutes, until fragrant.

5 Add a splash of the water and the tamarind paste and salt and bring to a boil.

6 Reduce the heat and simmer for 10 minutes.

7 Add the fish head, okra, tofu, tomatoes, remaining water and coconut milk and simmer until the fish is cooked, about 10 minutes.

8 Turn off the heat and serve garnished with coriander leaves.

TASTING NOTES

Beautifully combining elements from across the continent, Peranakan fish head curry has a sour-spice flavour that's reminiscent of *tom yum* (Thai seafood soup) and is more liquid than traditional Indian curry. Eschew the Indian hand-to-mouth eating method; you'll want a spoon. The flavour comes from tamarind paste while the spice comes from chillies, the former acting as a brake on the latter, giving this dish a slow burn. Though the fish head is the dish's star, the fried tofu soaks up most of the flavour and okra adds texture. For extra authenticity – or to impress your friends – try eating an eyeball. They are crunchy on the outside and gooey on the inside! ● *by Joshua Samuel Brown*

YOU'LL NEED

1 tbs vegetable oil

2 medium onions, peeled and diced

450g (1lb) stewing or braising beef, cubed

2 garlic cloves, peeled and minced

3 tbs Hungarian paprika

1 tsp caraway seeds, ground

pinch of cayenne pepper

2–3 cups water

400g (14oz) potatoes, peeled and cubed

3 medium carrots, peeled and cubed

salt, to taste

crusty bread or fresh egg noodles, to serve

ORIGINS

Goulash was the staple meal of herders who drove cattle on Hungary's plains as far back as the 9th century. The herdsmen would cook the stew in iron kettles over a fire, supposedly using animals that couldn't make the trip, until it was almost dry so it could be stored in sheep's-stomach bags and later reconstituted with water. Paprika was not considered a crucial ingredient until the Turks introduced the spice to the country in the 18th century.

SERVES 4

HUNGARY

GOULASH

Hungary's national dish – a hearty feast of tender beef chunks and root vegetables flavoured with local paprika – has been sustaining everyone from Magyar cattle-herders to restaurant-goers for generations.

METHOD

1 Heat the oil in a heavy-based casserole pan. Add the onions and cook until soft and golden.

2 Add the beef and stir-fry until the meat is no longer pink and any liquid has evaporated.

3 Add the garlic, paprika, caraway seeds and cayenne pepper and fry for a few minutes to coat the beef. Add enough water to just cover the meat. Bring to a boil.

4 Add the potatoes and carrots.

5 Turn down the heat to a simmer and cook the goulash for at least an hour or until the beef is tender and the potatoes and carrots are cooked.

6 Season the soup as required with salt and more caraway.

7 Serve with crusty bread or fresh egg noodles.

TIP *An easy dish to replicate at home, but do try to use Hungarian paprika, which gives the dish its characteristic warmth and bittersweet taste. Chop the meat and vegetables to the same approximate sizes for even cooking.*

TASTING NOTES

Long, cold winters in Hungary require nourishing slow-cooked foods such as goulash, which goes perfectly with noodles or dumplings. Not to be confused with that other Hungarian staple *pörkölt* (a dry-fried meat stew), a bowl of goulash is a one-pot wonder of beef and vegetables that becomes a complete meal when cooked with egg noodles called *csipetke*. Unlike the smoky Spanish version or the mild, generic versions found in most supermarkets, the Hungarian paprika lends an intense red-capsicum flavour and deep-red colour to the dish. It comes in mild, sweet, semisweet and hot varieties, depending on the type of capsicum, but even the hot versions will have a more complex aroma and taste than cayenne or chilli powder. ● *by Johanna Ashby*

YOU'LL NEED

1 tbs sesame oil

320g (11oz) pork, preferably pork rashers or pork belly, chopped

about 2 cups *kimchi* – the older and funkier the better

½ onion, peeled and sliced

3 garlic cloves, peeled and crushed

2 tbs *gochujang* (hot pepper paste)

3 cups hot water

200g (7oz) tofu, chopped

¼ cup chopped spring onions (scallions)

steamed rice, to serve

ORIGINS

Despite being built to last, even *kimchi* can pass its best, but that doesn't mean it's ready for retirement. *Kimchi jjigae* was designed with recycling in mind using leftover *kimchi*. The stew is ideal on crisp, cold days and is being prescribed (non-medically of course) to clear up colds. Despite its heat – both of the temperature and spice varieties – you'll find it on menus nationwide even in the steamiest summer months.

SERVES 4

KOREA

KIMCHI JJIGAE

This fiery stew features the country's most famous ingredient, *kimchi*, boiled up with scallions, onion, garlic and *gochujang* (red pepper paste), and topped off with pork, tofu or tinned tuna.

METHOD

1 Place a deep pan over a medium heat, add the sesame oil and heat briefly.

2 Add the pork and fry until lightly browned and any fat is slightly crispy.

3 Add the *kimchi* and cook for 2 minutes, stirring occasionally.

4 Add the sliced onion, crushed garlic and *gochujang* (more if your spice threshold is higher!)

5 Add 2 cups of the water, plus any juices from the *kimchi* and bring to the boil.

6 Partially remove the lid and reduce the heat, simmering for 20–30 minutes. Add more water if the broth begins to evaporate or is too pungent for your tastes.

7 Add the chopped tofu and simmer for a further 10 minutes.

8 Sprinkle on the chopped spring onions just before you remove the stew from the heat, and stir.

9 Serve the stew with steamed rice on the side – and keep a handkerchief handy!

TASTING NOTES

Like many of the country's stews, *kimchi jjigae* is served literally boiling hot, the broth still bubbling when it reaches your table. It's traditionally a communal dish, and while you'll often find it surrounded by the numerous *banchan* (side dishes) ubiquitous in Korean cuisine, it can also be ordered as a main meal with a simple side of rice at inexpensive lunchtime eateries. Stewed *kimchi* retains a touch of crunch and lends a complex flavour to the broth – you'll taste not only the ingredients added to the pan but also everything used to make the *kimchi* itself. To soften the heat, eat it with a little rice, or keep a stash of plain rice aside to chomp between slurps. ● *by Lucy Corne*

ORIGINS

Settlement in Iceland was rough, as Celtic and Viking descendants grappled with unforgiving weather and limited food choices. *Kjötsúpa* – a lamb soup with the hearty consistency of a stew – was an effective way to stretch meat rations by adding root vegetables and grains. Every family has their own version of the recipe, and subtle tweaks – barley instead of rice, turnips instead of beetroot (beets) – are part of the dish's heritage.

SERVES 4

ICELAND

KJÖTSÚPA

Sheep outnumber people on the island nation of Iceland, and they take centre-stage in the local cuisine. This meaty lamb stew is a classic family meal.

YOU'LL NEED

450g (1lb) lamb shoulder or
  leg, diced
salt and pepper, to taste
1 tbs oil
1 small onion, peeled and diced
1 celery stick, diced
½ cup rice
2 cups beef stock
200g (7oz) carrots, peeled
  and roughly chopped
200g (7oz) beetroot (beets) or
  swede (rutabagas), peeled
  and roughly chopped
200g (7oz) potatoes, roughly
  chopped

METHOD

1 Chop the lamb into small cubes, rub with salt and pepper and set aside.

2 In a large pan, saute the onion and celery in the oil until tender (around 15 minutes)

3 Add the lamb, rice, stock and 2 cups of water and bring to the boil.

4 Reduce the heat and simmer for 30 minutes, skimming foam off the top as necessary.

5 Add the remaining vegetables, simmer for 30 more minutes.

6 Season with salt and pepper to taste, and serve.

TASTING NOTES

If you're using Icelandic lamb, the first thing you'll notice as you tuck into your stew is that the flavour of the meat is slightly different to that of lamb raised elsewhere. Icelandic sheep are allowed to roam free in the countryside during the summer months, grazing on wild fields of angelica before being rounded up in October for slaughter. The mountain herb subtly imparts its fragrance to the meat, even when cooked, which adds a welcome earthy quality to the dish. Traditionally, preparations for a meal for four should yield plenty of leftovers – a good thing, because *kjötsúpa* tastes even better reheated the next day. ● *by Brandon Presser*

ORIGINS

Its name gives a vital clue, but no one can agree on the true story of *mapo tofu*. Yes, the recipe can be traced back to a small restaurant in Chengdu in 1862. Beyond that, discrepancies arise. *Mapo*, Chinese for 'pockmarked grandmother', refers to the restaurant owner who invented the dish. Or it refers to her pockmarked husband. Maybe no one was pockmarked, and this was a slur by local restaurant owners, understandably envious of the success of this deliciously groundbreaking combination of tofu and beef.

TASTING NOTES

Sichuanese food is renowned for being hot and spicy, but that's an over-simplification of this incredibly sophisticated cuisine. Chefs aim to create dishes that artfully combine basic flavours of sour, pungent, hot, sweet, bitter, aromatic and salty. But it's *ma*, the disconcerting, then compelling, and finally addictive numbing effect of Sichuan peppercorns that gives the cuisine its edge. And *ma la* – that tingling sensation combined with fiery chilli heat – is Sichuan's signature combination. *Ma* has been described as like touching the terminals of a nine-volt battery to your tongue, or having mouthful of Pop Rocks. The Sichuanese say that once you're accustomed to it, if you go without for too long your mouth starts to feel bland. Proceed with caution – this is powerful stuff. ● *by Janine Eberle*

SERVES 4

SICHUAN, CHINA

MAPO TOFU

Silky, soothing tofu on a background of fiery, mouth-numbing, *umami*-rich sauce – this bowl is a flavour and texture sensation. But beware: it's truly addictive.

YOU'LL NEED

1½ tsp Sichuan peppercorns
1 tsp sea salt
1 tsp cornflour (cornstarch)
2 tbs vegetable oil
2 tsp ground red chillies (optional)
230g (8oz) ground beef
3 garlic cloves, sliced
1 tbs fresh ginger, sliced
1 tbs fermented black beans, rinsed, drained and chopped
2 tbs broad bean chilli paste (*dou ban jiang*)
2 tbs Shaoxing (Chinese cooking) wine
1 tbs dark soy sauce
¼ cup chicken stock
450g (1lb) silken tofu, drained and cut into 1cm (½in) cubes
¼ cup finely sliced spring onions (scallions)
steamed rice, to serve

METHOD

1 Heat 1 tsp of the peppercorns over a high heat until lightly smoking. Transfer to a mortar and pestle with ½ tsp of the sea salt, pound until finely ground and set aside. Lightly pound the remaining ½ tsp peppercorns and set aside.

2 Combine the cornflour with 2 tsp cold water in a small bowl and mix with a fork until smooth. Set aside.

3 Heat the oil in a wok over a high heat. Add the beef and cook, stirring, for 1 minute. Add the garlic, ginger and black beans and cook until fragrant, about 15 seconds. Add most of the lightly pounded peppercorns, chilli paste, wine, soy sauce, and chicken stock and bring to a boil. Pour in the cornflour mixture and cook for 30 seconds, until thickened.

4 Add the tofu carefully and spoon some sauce over it, being careful not to break it up too much. Cover the wok and simmer for 1 minute, just enough to warm the tofu through. Sprinkle with the remaining ground peppercorn and salt, and the spring onions.

5 Serve immediately in deep bowls with steamed rice.

YOU'LL NEED

6 large russet potatoes,
   peeled and cut into ½cm
   (¼in) thick batons
canola or vegetable oil
salt
600g (1⅓lb) cheese curds

For the gravy

2 tbs cornflour (cornstarch)
6 tbs unsalted butter
¼ cup flour
2 garlic cloves, peeled and
   finely chopped
2½ cups beef stock
1 cup chicken stock
pepper

ORIGINS

Created after World War II,
poutine (pronounced poo-tsin)
was a thrifty way to make full
use of mealtime leftovers – old
potatoes, cheese rinds and
the broth boiled from chicken
bones. Today, this thoroughly
Québecois dish has become
a hero of Canadian cuisine,
and has evolved from *grand-
maman's* surefire way to keep
warm on winter nights into
a perennial after-hours
snack to soak up all those
rounds of Labatt.

QUÉBEC, CANADA

POUTINE

SERVES 4

The ultimate salty indulgence – French fries and cheese under a velvety gravy duvet. Enjoyed at *casse-croûtes* (snack bars) across Canada, the popularity of *poutine* has made it the country's unofficial national dish.

METHOD

1 In a large bowl, soak the cut potatoes in cold water for 30 minutes. Drain and pat dry with a cloth.

2 Preheat the oil in the deep-fryer to 170°C (340°F) and line a baking tray with paper towels.

3 Carefully put the potatoes in the fryer basket and cook for 5–6 minutes.

4 Drain and spread the fried potatoes on the baking tray until they cool.

5 Increase the fryer temperature to 180°C (350°F) and return the potatoes to the fryer for 1–2 minutes, until they're golden and crispy. (You may want to complete this second fry just before serving.)

6 Drain the fries again on the baking tray and set aside (or keep warm in the oven).

7 For the gravy, dissolve the cornflour in 2 tbs water, then set aside.

8 Melt the butter in a pan. Add the flour and stir for 5 minutes, until golden.

9 Add the garlic and stir for 30 seconds, then add the stocks and stir until boiling.

10 Stir in the cornflour and pepper to taste for 4–5 minutes, until the sauce thickens.

11 Season the fries with salt. Serve in bowls topped with cheese curds and brown sauce.

TASTING NOTES

Haute twists on *poutine* include gourmet toppings such as smoked meat, sliced foie gras, and even seafood in the far-eastern parts of the province, but the uninitiated should keep things classic. If you'd like to simplify the dish even further (or you don't have access to a fryer), you can substitute the hand-cut potatoes with frozen French fries; the most important part of the dish is the inclusion of homemade gravy (called *la sauce brune*) served piping hot to melt the cheese curds. To maximise the tasting experience, let the *poutine* sit for 5 minutes before digging in to let the three tiers – fries, cheese and sauce – start melding together to form the perfect salt bomb. ● *by Brandon Presser*

ORIGINS

Quinoa cultivation dates back millennia in South America, but because the Spanish favoured cereal crops for sustenance after they arrived in the New World, a cloak of the unknown hung over this superfood until the late 20th century. This stew, however, embraces both indigenous and conquistador influences – similar spicy quinoa dishes would have been consumed by the pre-Columbian civilisations, but without the Spanish-introduced garlic and tomato.

YOU'LL NEED

2 tbs olive oil
2 cups peeled and chopped onions
1 cup sliced celery
½ cup peeled and sliced carrots
3 garlic cloves, peeled and minced
3 tsp ground cumin
1 tsp chilli powder
1 tsp ground coriander
pinch of cayenne pepper
2 tsp dried oregano
1 cup cooked chickpeas, rinsed
1 cup diced green (bell) pepper
400g (14oz) canned chopped tomatoes with juice
1 bay leaf
2 cups vegetable stock
400g (14oz) fresh tomatoes.
2 tsp finely chopped fresh coriander (cilantro) leaves
3 tbs red wine vinegar
½ cup quinoa
1 cup water

SERVES 4

BOLIVIA AND PERU

QUINOA STEW

A feisty chilli, chickpea, and garlic-infused tomato stew laden
to the gills with quinoa, this nutritious hearty hotpot has been
warming the cockles of Andean folks since the dawn of time.

METHOD

1 Heat the oil in a large heavy-based pan.
Saute the onions in the oil for 5 minutes.

2 Add the celery and carrots and cook for
5 minutes more.

3 Add the minced garlic and saute for a
further 2 minutes.

4 Add the cumin, chilli powder, coriander,
cayenne pepper and oregano and mix in well.

5 Add the chickpeas, green pepper, canned
tomatoes, bay leaf and stock and bring to
a boil.

6 Reduce the heat and simmer for 15 minutes.

7 Add first the fresh tomatoes and then the
fresh coriander and red wine vinegar towards
the end of the cooking time.

8 As the stew is cooking, prepare the quinoa.
Rinse the quinoa thoroughly, place it in a pan,
then add the water and cook over a medium
heat, covered, for 15 minutes. Remove from
the heat and set aside.

9 Serve by dividing the stew into bowls and
adding 2–3 heaped tablespoons of quinoa
to each.

TASTING NOTES

Credit to the Andeans: few other regions of the world would bother to concoct what is first
and foremost a belly-filler and devote so much attention to the seasoning. The simmered-
soft quinoa (white quinoa is generally preferred by Peruvians and Bolivians) is the body of this
dish but ideally you want to grab a spoonful with the tomato-doused chickpea-rich vegetable
taste of the stew mixed in. The garlic, the herbs and the spice assail your senses a second
later. To appreciate this dish to the maximum, try it on a bus-journey break in a middle-of-
nowhere eatery high on the Andean plains. You'll walk in shivering, but after the old *abuela*
(grandmother) has doled you out a bowl of this you'll feel heart-warmed. ● *by Luke Waterson*

ORIGINS

The roots of Moroccan cuisine lie in the spices of Arabia, the tastes of Andalusia in Spain and the produce of Morocco. Spices such as cumin, ginger, cinnamon and coriander are perfect to complement the flavours, but the food is never chilli-hot, and fresh herbs add a bright burst of flavour. Traditionally, the conical-lidded earthenware tagine that gives the dish its name is cooked over coals – you'll see rows of them bubbling away at roadside cafes. Every restaurant will serve some kind of *loubia* dish, often as a starter.

YOU'LL NEED

230g (8oz) red kidney beans, soaked overnight
1 celery stick
1 bay leaf
6 sprigs of parsley
4 sprigs of fresh thyme
400g (14oz) canned chopped tomatoes
2 tbs olive oil
1 tsp sugar, to taste
1 large onion, peeled and chopped
2 garlic cloves, peeled and crushed with a little salt
1 red chilli, seeded and chopped
2 red (bell) peppers, seeded and chopped
1 tsp paprika
½ tsp ground cumin
½ tsp cinnamon
salt and pepper, to taste
handful each of fresh mint, parsley and coriander (cilantro) leaves, chopped
harissa, to serve
crusty bread, to serve

SERVES 2

MOROCCO
RED BEAN TAGINE

Hearty red kidney beans in a spicy tomato sauce with plenty of fresh mint and coriander: here is a bowlful of the quintessential Moroccan *loubia* (bean) dish taken to new heights.

METHOD

1 Drain the soaked beans, cover with fresh water (do not add salt) and bring to the boil. Simmer for 10 minutes and drain again.

2 Cover with fresh water (again, no salt), add the celery, bay leaf, parsley and thyme and bring to the boil. Simmer for about an hour until the beans are tender.

3 To make the sauce, put the canned tomatoes into a pan, add 1 tbs olive oil and simmer uncovered for about 20 minutes, until thick. Taste and add sugar if necessary.

4 Heat the oven to 180°C (350°F).

5 In a tagine or casserole dish, heat the remaining oil and add the onion, garlic, chilli, red peppers, paprika, cumin and cinnamon. Cook gently for 5 minutes.

6 Discard the bay leaf, celery stick, parsley and thyme from the beans. Drain, but reserve some of the cooking water.

7 Add the beans and tomato sauce to the casserole, season with salt and pepper, then cover and cook in the oven for about an hour, stirring occasionally. If it gets too dry, add a little of the reserved bean cooking water.

8 Check the seasoning and stir in the fresh herbs. Serve in bowls with harissa and crusty bread.

TASTING NOTES

Sitting down at a pavement cafe in a busy *medina* (old city) souk is a feast for the senses. Donkeys pass by while cats eye the butcher, men sell live chickens, women cook sheets of filo-like pastry, there's a cartful of mint, a pile of glistening oranges, a basket of duck eggs, and doughnuts tied up with a loop of palm frond. This dish brings the flavours of Morocco to the table with the earthiness of the kidney beans, ripe fullness of the tomatoes, warmth of the paprika and the tantalising spike of fresh mint and coriander (cilantro). Team with the heat of harissa – a condiment made of red chillies and (bell) peppers – add some crusty bread, and you have the perfect bowl of healthy fare. *Bismillah!* ● *by Helen Ranger*

YOU'LL NEED

1 cup dried chickpeas
450g (1lb) chicken on bone or
  beef chuck, chopped
200g (7oz) chorizo, sliced
olive oil
1 large onion, chopped
4 garlic cloves, chopped
2 tomatoes, chopped
1 red or green (bell) pepper,
  seeded and chopped
1 tsp paprika
1 tsp dried thyme
1 tsp dried oregano
salt and pepper
1 cup chicken stock
2–3 potatoes, sliced (optional)
  or rice, to serve

ORIGINS

Born from a way to use up
leftovers, *ropa vieja* wears its
humble beginnings in its very
name – meaning 'old clothes'
in Spanish. One origin tale tells
the story a poor man so hard
up that in a fit of desperation
to feed his family he cooked
up a stew using – you guessed
it – his old clothes. Praying
over the pot, he found his pleas
answered as the pile of laundry
turned into a hearty stew.

SERVES 4

CANARY ISLANDS, SPAIN

ROPA VIEJA

Whether you opt for a communal dish to share tapas-style, or tuck into your own bowl of this tasty chickpea stew, *ropa vieja* is high on the must-try list of Canarian cuisine.

METHOD

1 Soak the chickpeas in water overnight. Drain and rinse.

2 Bring a large pan of water to the boil and add the chickpeas and the chicken or beef. Simmer until the chickpeas soften and the meat is thoroughly cooked, about an hour.

3 Remove and shred the meat and drain the cooked chickpeas.

4 Dry-fry the chorizo lightly in a large pan for a minute or two, then set aside.

5 Heat a splash of olive oil in the pan and fry the onion until it begins to brown.

6 Add the chopped garlic, tomatoes, peppers, paprika, thyme, oregano and a pinch of salt and pepper.

7 Add the stock, chickpeas, chorizo and shredded meat and stir over a medium heat for 5 minutes.

8 Deep-fry the sliced potatoes (if using), until golden.

9 Serve the *ropa vieja* in bowls, topped with crispy fried potatoes or with steamed rice on the side.

TASTING NOTES

Ropa vieja is one of those dishes for which everyone has their own recipe, and as you travel from island to island, town to town, you'll quickly discover that no two batches of 'old clothes' are the same. But whether the dish is spiced up with cumin, topped with chorizo, loaded with garlic or piled high with leftover meat there's one thing it should always boast – a marvellous coming together of textures that has you reaching for spoonful after spoonful. The Canaries are most often associated with sand and sun but there's really no finer way to enjoy a dish of *ropa vieja* than in a misty *pueblo* tucked away in the mountains, glass of sweet local wine in hand. ● *by Lucy Corne*

ORIGINS

Throughout Latin America, *sancocho* refers to a traditional stew adapted from the Spanish *cocido*, a chickpea-based soup prepared with meat and vegetables. (The word *sancocho* also comes from Spain via the verb *sancochar*, which means 'to parboil'.) *Cocido* dates back at least to a dish prepared by Sephardic Jews in the Middle Ages, but the earliest *sancochos* in Latin America are said to have evolved from the cooking of immigrating Canary Islanders. Today, *sancocho de gallina* is the national dish of Panama.

TASTING NOTES

Every *sancocho* recipe is a little different. But it usually consists of a meat-based broth (often poultry, but also pork, beef and sometimes fish) into which are mixed big chunks of potato, cassava, plantain and other less starchy vegetables such as corn, tomato or spring onions (scallions). Seasoning and spices give the final bowl its flavour and its colour, which can vary from light brown to bright green, yellow or orange. Rice is the standard accompaniment, either mixed in entirely or dipped into the broth spoonful by spoonful. *Sancocho* is rarely spicy, so added *ají picante* (hot sauce) or an optional topping of fresh coriander (cilantro), onion and squeezed lime definitely enhances the dish. A side of sliced avocado is common in Colombia – and delicious. ● *by Ethan Gelber*

SERVES 4

PANAMA

SANCOCHO DE GALLINA

Latin America's most beloved meat-and-veg soup, *sancocho* is like a typical Sunday family event – warmth, comfort, care and conviviality – based in a bowl. It's a great hangover remedy, too.

YOU'LL NEED

2 garlic cloves, minced
1 tsp dried oregano
½ tsp black pepper
3 tbs fresh *culantro* (Mexican
   or sawtooth coriander),
   chopped; or substitute
   coriander (cilantro)
3 tsp olive oil
1 chicken, jointed
1 large onion, chopped
4 cups chicken stock
1kg (2lb 2oz) starchy
   vegetables (potato, yam,
   cassava, plantain), peeled
   and chopped
2 ears corn, cut into 2in pieces
salt, to taste
fresh coriander (cilantro)
steamed rice, to serve
1 avocado, sliced, to serve
lime wedges, to serve

METHOD

1 Combine the garlic, oregano, pepper, *culantro* and 1 tsp olive oil. Rub over the chicken and leave to marinate for 10 minutes.

2 Put the remaining olive oil in a heavy-bottomed pan over a medium heat. Add the chicken, cover and cook for 5 minutes.

3 Add the onion and enough stock to cover the chicken. Bring to the boil, then reduce the heat. Simmer until the chicken is cooked through (about 20 minutes).

4 Increase the heat to medium, add the starchy vegetables and cook until fork tender (20–40 minutes). Keep adding stock to cover the vegetables.

5 Add the corn and cook until tender, 15 minutes.

6 Add salt to taste and sprinkle with coriander.

7 Serve in bowls with steamed rice, a side of avocado and lime wedges.

ORIGINS

Some say stovies got their name from the French *étuvée*, which means braised, others say it's simply because this humble dish is cooked on top of the stove. Either way, stovies divide opinion; there's no accepted recipe and heated arguments flare up over how they should be cooked and eaten – evidence enough of their deep-seated place in Scottish culture. No one argues about a dish they don't care about. There's even a World Stovies Championship, for the truly brave.

SCOTLAND

STOVIES

From a modest combination of ingredients comes stovies, one of Scotland's best-loved dishes, a deeply satisfying, belly-filling, soul-soothing bowl of leftover lamb, potatoes and onions.

YOU'LL NEED

2 tbs leftover lamb dripping
3 onions, peeled and roughly sliced
6 medium-sized floury potatoes, peeled and roughly chopped
2 cups stock
340g (12oz) leftover roast lamb
salt and pepper
oatcakes, to serve

METHOD

1 Put the lamb dripping in a large pan and heat until melted.

2 Add the onions to the pot and cook slowly for about 20 minutes until they begin to caramelise.

3 Add the potatoes, stir well, then add enough stock to cover everything.

4 Simmer for 20 minutes or until the potatoes are almost falling apart. Stir well so that they begin to break up.

5 Add the lamb and continue to simmer until the potatoes have soaked up all the stock.

6 Season with salt and pepper and stir until the ingredients are well combined.

7 Serve in bowls with oatcakes on the side.

TASTING NOTES

Mashed up into a pulp and simply presented in a bowl with a spoon, stovies will never win a beauty contest, but their slapdash appearance is instantly forgotten after the first soothing mouthful. There's an intense pleasure in scooping up a spoonful of this soft lamb and potato mix and just succumbing to the sense of well-being it evokes. Typically cooked on a Monday to use up any meat, gravy and vegetables left over from the Sunday roast, stovies have a depth of flavour that belies their simple ingredients and for many Scottish people, this is simply the taste of 'home'. Traditionally lamb was used but beef, pork, sausages or corned beef make the occasional appearance too, as does turnip and swede. ● *by Etain O'Carroll*

ORIGINS

Like everything in Cape
Malay culture, *bredie* has its
roots in various lands. Cape
Malay cuisine was brought to
South Africa with Southeast
Asian slaves and adapted to
incorporate local ingredients.
The word *bredie* – Afrikaans
for 'stew' – is thought to stem
from a Portuguese/Malay
creole word referring to edible
greens. These days the main
base for the stew is tomatoes,
though a lesser-known recipe
uses *waterblommetjie*, Cape
pondweed. You'll only find this
version in the winter months
from June to August, when the
pondweed is in flower.

YOU'LL NEED

2 tbs butter
800g (1¾lb) lamb shank,
    shoulder or neck, chopped
    into 4cm (1½in) pieces
2 onions, peeled and roughly
    chopped
3 garlic cloves, peeled and
    finely chopped
6 tomatoes, chopped
1 tsp sugar
1 tsp paprika
2 cinnamon sticks
½ tsp ground cloves
¼ tsp chilli powder
2 cardamom pods
3cm (1¼in) piece of fresh
    ginger, peeled and finely
    chopped or grated
1½ cups stock
4–5 medium potatoes,
    chopped
salt and pepper, to taste
fresh parsley, chopped, or
    cooked rice, to serve

SERVES 4

WESTERN CAPE, SOUTH AFRICA

TOMATO BREDIE

**You can soak it up with rice or mop it up with
a freshly cooked *roti* – either way, this fragrant and
filling lamb stew is perfect for cheering up grey days.**

METHOD

1 Melt the butter in a large pan. Brown the lamb in batches, then set aside.

2 Fry the onions in the same pan, for about 15 minutes, until they begin to brown, then add the garlic and cook until fragrant.

3 Add the chopped tomatoes, sugar, paprika, cinnamon sticks, cloves, chilli, cardamom and fresh ginger.

4 Let the mixture simmer for 2–3 minutes, then add the stock. Bring to the boil and add the lamb.

5 Reduce the heat, cover and simmer for 2 hours, stirring occasionally.

6 Add the potatoes, season to taste and cook for a further 30 minutes or until the potatoes are soft.

7 Serve on a bed of rice or simply in a bowl topped with a sprinkle of parsley.

TASTING NOTES

It can be infuriatingly tricky to find dedicated Cape Malay restaurants in South Africa, but stumbling across the odd dish hidden among steaks and seafood on a standard restaurant menu isn't unheard of. Tomato *bredie* comes in all shapes and sizes – matronly measures filling bowls in backwater towns and sometimes even refined portions plated to perfection and elevated to fine-dining standards. Recipes likewise vary, with each cook closely guarding their personal spice blend, but what you'll always find is a tangy tomato gravy enriched with a light lacing of lamb fat. Chunks of tender lamb take on subtle Asian aromatics of clove, ginger, cardamom and cinnamon, sometimes with a hint of chilli heat. ● *by Lucy Corne*

YOU'LL NEED

680g (1½lb) lamb neck on the bone
1 onion, peeled and roughly chopped
sea salt
1 medium swede (rutabaga), chopped
2 carrots, chopped
3 large potatoes, chopped
2 parsnips, chopped
2 large leeks, outer leaves removed, chopped into thick rounds
fresh parsley, chopped
crusty bread and Welsh cheese, to serve

ORIGINS

Considered by many to be the national dish of Wales, cawl (pronounced *cowl*) has been eaten across the country for centuries. It's a fairly typical country stew based on easily available ingredients simmered slowly in a pan; its intense flavours and deeply satisfying nature are what make it stand out from the crowd. The exact recipe varies from family to family, handed down through the generations, and can be made with lamb, mutton, beef or bacon.

SERVES 4

WALES

WELSH CAWL

A bowl of hearty goodness, cawl is a traditional Welsh stew made from lamb and winter veg. Left to mature overnight these humble ingredients transform into something quite magical.

METHOD

1 Place the lamb and onion in a large pan. Cover with water and add salt.

2 Bring to the boil, then reduce the heat and simmer gently, skimming the top as necessary, for 2–3 hours until the meat is nearly falling off the bone.

3 Remove the meat from the pan, allow it to cool, then shred the meat from the bones and return it to the pan.

4 Add the chopped swede, carrots, potatoes and parsnips to the pan, season to taste and simmer for 15 minutes or until tender.

5 Add half the chopped leeks to the pan and simmer for 10 minutes before adding the remaining leeks.

6 Cover the pan, allow it to cool and then put in the fridge overnight.

7 When ready to eat, heat the cawl until it simmers, then ladle into bowls and garnish with chopped parsley. Serve with crusty bread and Welsh cheese.

TASTING NOTES

Sodden from a day out walking in the Welsh hills, the sky low and daylight fading, you finally see the twinkling lights of the village pub in the valley below. As you descend towards it, your stomach begins to rumble and thoughts of a cosy fire and hot dinner take residence in your mind and are impossible to shift. Inside the pub, you're served a steaming bowl of cawl with melt-in-the-mouth lamb, vegetables that have been slow-cooked to develop a subtle sweetness, and a rich broth that warms from within, evoking a sense of profound satisfaction. Somehow, a bowl of well-made cawl has a way of putting everything to rights at the end of a long grey day. ● *by Etain O'Carroll*

DESSERTS

OK, it's not rare for desserts to come in a bowl, but for some there's simply no other option. From the weird – Malaysia's bright green spaghetti-like *cendol* – to the simply wonderful, such as the classic English Eton mess, these are the desserts that keep us coming back for spoonful after spoonful, grateful for the difficulty of portion control when dining *à la bowl*.

🥣 Easy   🥣🥣 Medium   🥣🥣🥣 Hard

ORIGINS

The berries of the Amazonian açaí palm were barely known outside the Amazon until the 1970s. In the following decade the legendary Brazilian ju-jitsu founder Carlos Gracie popularised açaí bowl in Rio de Janeiro, and it wasn't long before local surfers adopted the snack as the perfect post-session pick-me-up. In the early noughties, the first batch of açaí pulp winged its way to the USA, and Hawaii and Southern California became the first places where açaí bowl found a foreign home. It's now enjoyed from Sydney to London.

YOU'LL NEED

2 heaped tbs freeze-dried açaí powder or about 110g (4oz) slightly thawed açaí pulp

2 heaped tbs milled seeds (chia, flax, sunflower etc)

⅔ cup almond milk, coconut milk, coconut water or apple juice

1½ cups frozen blueberries and/or sliced banana

For the toppings

⅔ cup fresh seasonal berries and/or figs

1 ripe banana, sliced

4 tbs muesli or oats

2 tbs seeds or other toppings (try flaxseed, chia seeds, shredded coconut, jungle peanuts and/or bee pollen)

SERVES 2

BRAZIL

AÇAÍ BOWL

It looks like ice cream, and tastes like ice cream, but this tropical Brazilian superfood snack couldn't be healthier. Refreshingly cool and satisfyingly filling, it's heaven in a bowl.

METHOD

1 Blend the açaí powder/pulp with the milled seeds, liquid and frozen fruit.

2 Add more liquid until it reaches the desired consistency, according to your personal taste.

3 Transfer the mixture to a breakfast bowl.

4 Top the mixture with fresh berries and/or figs, sliced banana, muesli (or oats) and seeds, in whichever combination you prefer.

5 Serve immediately.

TIP *Choose the liquid to blend with the açaí powder/pulp to suit your personal taste; the milkier the liquid, the creamier the mixture will be.*

TASTING NOTES

Waking up on a hot, sticky morning by the Brazilian seaside, the cool combination of berries and nuts in an açaí bowl provide the ultimate wake-up call, with a health kick to boot. With a similar consistency to lightly defrosted gelato, the rich, deep-purple açaí pulp or powder mixture forms the basis of this attractive tropical dish. Traditional Brazilian toppings include sliced banana and a sprinkling of granola, but Western cafes usually also offer an additional range of healthy toppings such as blueberries, shaved coconut, seeds and nuts. While the açaí mixture, which tastes a little bit like blackberries mixed with dark chocolate, is deliciously moreish by itself, the crunch of nuts provides delightful texture. ● *by Sarah Reid*

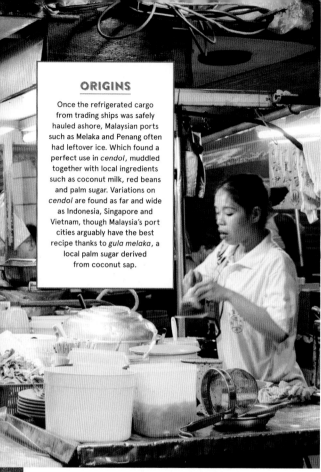

ORIGINS

Once the refrigerated cargo from trading ships was safely hauled ashore, Malaysian ports such as Melaka and Penang often had leftover ice. Which found a perfect use in *cendol*, muddled together with local ingredients such as coconut milk, red beans and palm sugar. Variations on *cendol* are found as far and wide as Indonesia, Singapore and Vietnam, though Malaysia's port cities arguably have the best recipe thanks to *gula melaka*, a local palm sugar derived from coconut sap.

YOU'LL NEED

100g (3½oz) rice flour
100g (3½oz) mung bean flour
1 tbs tapioca flour
¼ tsp pandan essence
4–5 tbs *gula melaka* (or other palm sugar)
80g (3oz) canned red beans
⅞ cup coconut milk
300g (10½oz) ice

TASTING NOTES

Green noodles and red beans, syrup-soaked ice, and occasional toppings from mango to durian, the pungent 'King of Fruits' – yes, *cendol* looks strange, but this frosty sundae is truly enticing on humid days in Malaysia. Street food hubs such as Melaka's Jonker Walk have numerous outlets, from dedicated dessert parlours to roadside stalls where *cendol* is whisked together on plastic tables. From the first spoonful, the coconut milk's creamy notes are freshened by ice that has been finely crushed to melt in the mouth. Syrup of *gula melaka* (unrefined, low-glycemic index, and almost good for you) delivers a caramel-scented sugar rush. Jelly-like noodles and soft red beans add texture, beautifully washed down by the mellow sweetness and melting ice. ● *by Anita Isalska*

SERVES 2

MALAYSIA

CENDOL

Sure, it resembles an alien's brains, but this tangle of
green noodles, palm sugar and slushy ice recalls Malaysia's
seafaring history. And it's pure refreshment in a bowl.

METHOD

1 Combine the three flours in a bowl.

2 Simmer three-fifths of a cup of water in a
pan, then take it off the heat. Add the flour
mix little by little, while stirring.

3 When it becomes a smooth, thick paste
(add more water drop by drop if necessary),
add the pandan essence and stir.

4 Place a couple of ice cubes and some cold
water into a large bowl.

5 Press the paste through a potato ricer or
colander to form green noodles, allowing them
to drop straight into the ice water.

6 Place the *gula melaka* into a small bowl and
add hot water, drop by drop, until you have
just enough to create a smooth, runny syrup,
then set aside.

7 Drain the noodles and split them between
two bowls.

8 Place half of the red beans into each bowl,
and pour coconut milk on top of each.

9 Pass the remaining ice cubes through an ice
shaver, or place them in a plastic bag and use
a rolling pin to crush them finely. Heap ice on
top of both bowls.

10 Pour the *gula melaka* syrup on to the
crushed ice, and serve immediately with
spoons (and plenty of napkins).

NOTE *If you don't want to make your own
noodles, you can substitute ready-made sweet
potato or rice noodles (cooked and cooled).*

ORIGINS

While *pho* and *bo bun* have conquered the world, Vietnamese desserts have been left languishing sweetly in the background. It's surprising, because in their homeland they're adored, and multitude. *Che*, just one variety, is not quite a dessert, and not quite a drink, akin to porridge, and a little like a sweet soup. In countless shapes, sizes and colours, served everywhere from roving street sellers to glitzy flashing-light chains, *che* can be served hot or cold, but in the heat of southern Vietnam it mostly comes with crushed ice.

SERVES 2

VIETNAM

CHE CHUOI

Baby bananas and tender tapioca simmered in coconut milk to make a sweet stew – comfort guaranteed, served warm or chilled.

YOU'LL NEED

¼ cup tapioca pearls
1 cup canned unsweetened
coconut milk
½ cup sugar
pinch sea salt
1 pandan leaf, slightly bruised
and tied in a knot (optional)
2 ripe baby or finger bananas
or plantains, peeled and
diced
toasted sesame seeds

METHOD

1 Soak the tapioca pearls in cold water overnight or for at least an hour prior to cooking.

2 Drain the soaked tapioca pearls. Bring the coconut milk and 1 cup water to the boil. Reduce the heat to medium-low, stir in the tapioca pearls, sugar, salt and pandan leaf, and cook until the tapioca pearls are translucent, 15–20 minutes.

3 Add the banana and cook for 10 minutes more. Remove and discard the pandan leaf.

4 Divide between bowls and garnish each with a sprinkle of sesame seeds. Serve hot, at room temperature, or chilled.

TASTING NOTES

The variety of *che* described here, bananas cooked with tapioca and coconut, is a simple one. *Che* can include any number of components – beans, lotus seeds, water chestnuts, corn, brightly coloured jellies, fruits such as longan, durian and lychee – cooked in sugar and often layered in a glass. An afternoon *che* catch-up among friends is as common as a coffee date in the West (though the Vietnamese love their *ca phe* too), and visiting a *che* stand is a quintessential street food experience. Point out your chosen ingredients – sweet potato, black beans, seaweed jelly, glutinous rice dumplings – see them layered into a glass or plastic bowl, pull up a child-sized stool, and indulge in the wash of cooling sweetness. ● *by Janine Eberle*

YOU'LL NEED

300g (10½oz) chocolate
  – milk, dark, white or a
  mixture
8 small balloons
ice cream, berries, whipped
  cream, custard or other
  filling of choice

ORIGINS

Like its culinary cousin the
ice-cream cone, the chocolate
dessert bowl emerged as a 'why
not?' gimmick created by clever
dessert chefs to enliven the
serving of popular but simple
sweets such as ice cream,
mousse and custard. Once found
exclusively in speciality dessert
shops and fancy restaurants,
a nifty trick involving ordinary
balloons has made the dish so
easy to create that the edible
chocolate bowl has become
common for kids' parties, dinner
soirées, and even – again, why
not? – routine snacking.

TASTING NOTES

Though some insist on finishing its contents before taking their first bite out of the chocolate
bowl itself, such finicky eaters are missing half the pleasure of this dish – namely the
textural interplay between the inner and outer desserts, of which there are many possible
combinations and varieties. Ice cream of any flavour works beautifully, keeping the bowl
well chilled to produce a lovely snap in counterpoint to the ice cream's smoothness.
Whipped cream with blueberries offers three distinct textures, as well as a pleasing note
of tartness. Chocolate mousse and custard are also excellent choices, and can be fully
assembled in advance and refrigerated – a drizzle of fruit syrup adds extra colour, flavour
and pizzazz. ● *by Joshua Samuel Brown*

EUROPE & NORTH AMERICA

CHOCOLATE DESSERT BOWL

SERVES 8

What could be sweeter than eating your favourite dessert? How about eating your favourite dessert and then eating the chocolate bowl that it came in?

METHOD

1 Blow up eight balloons, rinse and pat dry.

2 Line a baking tray with parchment paper.

3 Melt the chocolate in a microwave on high setting in 30-second bursts, stirring between each until the chocolate is melted and has a smooth consistency. Alternatively, melt the chocolate over a double boiler, placing a glass or metal bowl over a pan containing a little water on low heat and stirring regularly.

4 Let the chocolate cool for 5–10 minutes (it should be warm enough to work with without popping the balloons).

5 Using a tablespoon, create bases for the balloon bowls by measuring 2½cm-sized (1in) circles of chocolate on to paper-lined trays.

6 Holding a balloon by the knot, gently dip into the chocolate and swirl around until the bottom half of balloon is fully coated. Then press balloon onto the chocolate base.

7 Repeat with each balloon, then put the tray in the fridge for about 30 minutes to allow the chocolate to harden.

8 Remove from the fridge and gently deflate the balloons by pinching the top, creating a small hole and letting the air escape gently. Peel the balloons from the inside of the bowls.

9 Fill with your dessert of choice and serve.

YOU'LL NEED

2 egg whites
100g (3½oz) caster (superfine)
  sugar (plus extra)
1⅔ cups double (heavy) cream
450g (1lb) strawberries

ORIGINS

In one of the culinary world's
best origin tales, legend has it
that Eton mess was born when
an over-excited Labrador sat on
a picnic basket and crushed a
strawberry pavlova. Whatever its
history, the dish was seemingly
on sale in the tuck shop of
England's most prestigious
public (which, confusingly,
actually means private) school,
Eton College, in the 1930s and
was served at important cricket
matches and open days. How
it got into the hands of the riff
-raff remains a mystery.

SERVES 4

ENGLAND

ETON MESS

A quintessentially English summer dessert, Eton mess is a glorious combination of crushed meringue, fresh strawberries and whipped cream best served outdoors on a sunny day.

METHOD

1 Preheat the oven to 120°C (250°F).

2 Line a baking sheet with parchment paper.

3 Whisk the egg whites until stiff. Gradually add the sugar, a tablespoon at a time, and mix until thick and glossy.

4 Put 6 heaped spoonfuls of the egg mixture on to the baking tray. Place into the oven and bake for 90 minutes.

5 Turn off the oven, leaving the meringues inside until completely cooled.

6 Whip the cream lightly and sweeten to taste with more sugar.

7 Crush half of the strawberries to a pulp, then cut the other half into quarters.

8 Break the meringues into small pieces in a large bowl. Add the cream and crushed strawberries and mix gently.

9 Divide the mixture into four smaller bowls and garnish with the remaining strawberries.

TASTING NOTES

The success of this dish is largely due to its delicious jumble of textures, crispy yet chewy meringue, rich cream and succulent strawberries. It's a true crowd-pleaser that suits all age groups, can be whipped up in an instant (if you opt for shop-bought meringues), and is easily transportable. Somehow its slapdash presentation and simple flavours embody all that is wonderful about languid summer days spent strolling through parks or along sunny riverbanks, revelling in the warmth. Whether you just nip into the back garden on a summer's evening or lay out your spread on a Barbour picnic blanket by the cricket field, a big bowl of Eton mess adds a touch of glamour. Just beware of Labradors. ● *by Etain O'Carroll*

YOU'LL NEED

¼ cup basmati rice
2–3 cardamom pods
2 cups milk
1 tsp oil
½ cup slivered almonds
⅓ cup sugar
sultanas (golden raisins), to
   garnish (optional)

ORIGINS

Rice pudding has been enjoyed
in India for hundreds of years,
though the dessert – in a slightly
different guise – most likely
has its roots in ancient China,
where rice was first cultivated.
Enjoyed the world over, the
Indian version is infused with
cardamom and prepared with
lashings of whole milk. Known
as *kheer* in northern India and
payasam in the south, both
names are derived from Sanskrit
words meaning 'milk'.

INDIA

KHEER

**Sweet, cooling and fragrant, a bowl of *kheer* –
Indian rice pudding – is the perfect way to round
off a meal packed with subcontinental spice.**

METHOD

1 Rinse the rice then soak it in cold water for 20–30 minutes. Drain.

2 Crush the seeds from the cardamom pods with a pestle and mortar until they form a fine powder.

3 Heat the milk in a pan until it reaches the boil, then add the rice.

4 Cook on medium-low heat until the rice is very soft, 20–30 minutes.

5 Meanwhile, heat a small splash of vegetable or sunflower oil in a frying pan on medium heat and add the almonds (the oil should just coat the

nuts, not pool in the bottom of the pan).

6 Lightly toast the almonds until they just begin to brown, then remove from the heat.

7 When the rice is soft and squishy, add the sugar and cardamom and stir.

8 Cook for a further 5 minutes, or until the *kheer* starts to thicken.

9 Spoon into bowls and place in the fridge – it will continue to thicken as it cools.

10 When chilled, garnish with the toasted almonds and sultanas and serve.

TASTING NOTES

Kheer is enjoyed as an everyday dessert throughout India, but it's also a festive dish – a veritable bowl of celebration enjoyed at parties and weddings. Whether you're sampling it as the beat of a vibrant festival echoes around you, as a way to round off a simple Indian lunch in a street-side restaurant, or indeed in your own home, the dish offers a sweet spoonful of the subcontinent. The first thing you should dip into the bowl is not the spoon, but your nose, inhaling the sweet, creamy aroma with its exotic whiff of freshly crushed cardamom. Then tuck into a dish that is in equal parts cooling, rich, simple and delicious. ● *by Lucy Corne*

GLOSSARY

açaí Açaí is the grape-like fruit from a palm native to Central and South America. The pulp is made by removing the flesh from the seed, freezing then mashing it.

aji limo This is a medium-hot Peruvian chilli.

annatto-seed paste A paste made from annatto seeds, which imparts a bright orange colour and an earthy, slightly peppery taste to dishes.

arborio rice Arborio is a short grain rice with a high starch content, often used in risottos. Varieties include carnaroli and Vialone Nano.

bee hoon noodles Malaysian rice vermicelli noodles.

belacan Shrimp paste – pungent and salty. You can use anchovies mashed to a paste with a little water as a replacement.

besan flour Ground chickpeas (garbanzo beans), also known as gram flour.

bird's eye chilli A small chilli, technically medium in heat, but usually more than hot enough for most people.

bouquet garni A bundle of fresh herbs tied together with string, usually comprising thyme, bay leaf and parsley.

candlenuts A nut used to thicken Asian soups and curries. Try almonds, cashews or macadamias as

replacements. If you find candlenuts (Asian grocery stores stock them), they must be cooked before being eaten.

chia seed Small, nutrient-rich seeds of a tree native to Mexico and Guatemala, often used in health-focused cooking.

Chinese chives Also known as garlic chives. You can use chives as a mild substitute.

choclo Also called Peruvian corn or Cuzco corn, a large-kernel variety with a starchy texture and a taste similar to hominy.

chorizo A Portuguese or Spanish pork sausage, varieties range from mild to spicy. It is dry-cured, like a salami, and can be eaten uncooked or cooked. Substitute with pepperoni.

coriander Also known as cilantro, this leafy green herb is common in Mexican and Southeast Asian cooking.

culantro or **sawtooth coriander** A long-leafed herb, serrated as the name suggests. It can be replaced with coriander (cilantro), which is milder.

daikon A large, tubular, white radish, mild in flavour. Substitute with *jicama* or red radish (which is more pungent).

dashi A Japanese stock traditionally made from *kombu* (edible kelp) and dried shavings of tuna;

today, home cooks usually use liquid or powdered instant versions.

dried flat rice noodles Also known as flat rice stick noodles. Easy to find in an Asian grocery store. Other rice noodles could be used as a substitute.

edamame Immature soybeans, boiled or steamed in the pod and often served salted as a snack.

farro An ancient wheat grain similar to spelt.

galangal A rhizome, similar in appearance to ginger, though darker. Ginger can be used in its place, though it is much milder than galangal.

garam masala A sweet blend of spices – cardamom, cloves, cumin, pepper, among others.

ghee Clarified butter.

gochujang Korean fermented red pepper paste.

gram flour Ground chickpeas (garbanzo beans), also known as besan flour.

harissa A spicy North African paste made from a variety of chillies; recipes vary but it will often include garlic, salt and olive oil and spices such as cumin, coriander and caraway seeds and mint.

hoisin sauce A sweet, thick, dark sauce predominantly used in savoury cooking.

holy basil A pungent Asian herb with notes of anise, pepper and mint. Substitute with some Thai basil or sweet basil along with some mint.

hominy Whole corn kernels that have been soaked in a lye or lime solution, which softens the tough outer hulls and makes the grain expand, then washed to remove the hull, and often the germ.

jujube A small date-like fruit, also called red date, Chinese date or Korean date.

kabanosy Long sticks of smoked, dried Polish pork sausage.

kecap manis Indonesia's version of soy sauce, thicker and sweetened with palm sugar.

kimchi Pickled, fermented cabbage – a Korean staple.

manioc flour Also called cassava flour, this gluten-free flour is made from the tuberous root, also known as *yucca*, found in Central and Southern America.

matzo meal Matzo is an unleavened cracker-like bread made with flour and water, traditionally eaten at Passover. Matzo meal is made by finely grinding the matzo crackers into a breadcrumb-like consistency.

masa harina A flour made from hominy (hulled corn kernels).

New Mexico green chillies Mild green chillies.

nori An edible seaweed that is often shredded, dried and made into sheets, which are used to wrap sushi rolls.

nuoc cham Vietnamese dipping sauce made from fish sauce, lime juice, sugar, garlic and chilli.

palm sugar Sugar made from the sap of the palm tree. Use dark brown sugar in its place.

pandan leaves Long leaves from the pandan plant, used as a colouring and flavouring in Southeast Asian cuisine. Also available as an essence.

pico de gallo A Mexican salsa made by combining chopped tomato, onion, jalapeño pepper, coriander (cilantro) and lime juice.

plantains Related and similar in appearance to the banana, but needs to be cooked – often used in savoury dishes.

poblano chillies A common Mexican chilli, it's typically mild and used in a variety of ways. Also known as ancho chilli when dried.

pomegranate molasses A thick, dark, tart sauce made from reduced pomegranate juice. Use pomegranate or cranberry juice as a substitute.

purslane A wild green succulent, also known as duckweed or fatweed, slightly crunchy with a lemony taste.

queso fresco A salty white cheese used in Mexican and Andean cooking.

rocoto chilli A (usually) very hot chilli that is found in Central and South America.

salted radish Salted and preserved daikon radish. Available in Asian grocery stores.

sambal or **sambal oelek** Sambal is an Indonesian term for chilli paste; in *sambal oelek* the additional ingredients are usually simply salt and vinegar. Some versions may also contain diced onion, lemon or lime juice, garlic, or sugar.

sambal belacan A chilli paste made by blending together chillies, shrimp paste, lime and sugar. It's pungent and spicy. If you don't have shrimp paste, you could use anchovies to make it yourself. Or buy it ready-made from an Asian grocery store.

Shaoxing wine A traditional Chinese wine made from fermented rice, which is drunk as a beverage as well as used in cooking.

Sarawak laksa paste Quite different to the more common laksa pastes, this paste features *sambal belacan*, tamarind, garlic, galangal and lemongrass. Asam (aka Penang) laksa paste could be used in its place.

Scotch bonnet chillies A hot chilli common in the Carribbean. It can be replaced with habañero.

shiitake mushrooms Also known as Chinese mushrooms, these are commonly available dried in Asian grocery stores – soak them in hot water for half an hour before using them.

shoyu Japanese soy sauce.

shrimp paste Also known as *belacan*, this is a pungent and salty paste used as a base for curries and other sauces. Use anchovies mashed with a little water as a replacement.

smetana A kind of sour cream from Central and Eastern Europe, similar to *crème fraîche* and with a higher milkfat content than the generally lighter sour creams found elsewhere.

spiralizer An inexpensive kitchen gadget that allows you to make long spaghetti-like strands from vegetables such as courgettes (zucchini) and carrots.

star anise A star-shaped spice readily available in Asian grocery stores. Anise seed can be used as a substitute.

sumac A ground spice made from the dried fruit of the sumac shrub that is used in Middle Eastern cooking.

tahini paste Sesame seed paste.

tamarind concentrate or **paste** The pulp of the tamarind pod seeded and ready to use. It's sour and only slightly sweet. Use lemon juice for a souring effect in its place.

tapioca starch Tapioca flour, a common thickening agent. Use glutinous rice flour in its place.

Thai basil Milder than holy basil, more pungent than basil – but basil can be used as a substitute.

tempeh A traditional Indonesian soy product, made by fermenting and pressing soybeans. It has a firmer texture and a more distinct taste than tofu.

turmeric A rhizome like ginger, usually smaller, and beneath the dull orange peel, you'll find brilliant gold. Available fresh in Asian grocery stores, and as a ground spice almost everywhere.

umeboshi plum Pickled *ume* fruits, also called Japanese salt plums or pickled plums, extremely sour and salty.

urfa biber A Turkish dried chilli with a mild, smoky flavour.

wakame A sea vegetable or edible seaweed also known as sea mustard.

za'atar A spice mix made from thyme, sesame seeds and sumac, may also contain other herbs such as marjoram and oregano.

AUTHORS

Kate Armstrong Food connoisseur and lover of all things sweet. Capable chef. Global taste buds. Stomach of steel. Nothing – except oysters – is off her menu.

Johanna Ashby is a New York-based food and travel writer, always on the hunt for the best eating experiences from street food to fine dining and everything in between.

Brett Atkinson is a frequent traveller to Australia, Turkey and Southeast Asia, restaurant reviewer for www.viewauckland.co.nz, and incorrigible street food and craft beer fan.

Joe Bindloss was once a food critic for *Time Out*'s restaurant guides, specialising in food from Southeast Asia, China, Korea and the Indian subcontinent. He's currently a Lonely Planet Destination Editor.

Celeste Brash is a contributor to *The World is a Kitchen*, writer on food for Lonely Planet guidebooks and www. lonelyplanet.com, and an erstwhile professional cook.

Joshua Samuel Brown lives and dines in Taipei, Taiwan. An adventurous creator of interesting dishes, Joshua tweets his adventures on the road and in the kitchen at @josambro. Follow him online at www.josambro. com.

Austin Bush writes Thai food blog www. austinbushphotography. com, and for guidebooks

and magazines including *Saveur*, *Travel+Leisure Southeast Asia*, *Chile Pepper* and *DestinAsian*.

Lucy Corne has four passions: travel, food, writing and beer. She tries to combine the four wherever possible and is happiest at a street market, local delicacy in one hand and cold beer in the other. Lucy writes a popular blog on the South African beer scene.

Janine Eberle has worked for Lonely Planet for many years, both behind the desk and on the road. She's now a freelancer based in Paris where she writes about eating, drinking and other Parisian pastimes.

Carolyn B Heller is contributor to 50+ travel and food books for Lonely Planet, among others. She's eaten her way across more than 40 countries, and since relocating to Vancouver, Canada, she's been exploring the foods of her adopted nation, from bannock to butter tarts to beans.

Ethan Gelber is a voracious consumer of culture, including the edible kind. Between meals (his favourite time of day), he writes primarily about family travel, responsible and sustainable travel and keeping things local. He founded www. thetravelword.com and is the editorial director of the Family Travel Association.

Anita Isalska is a freelance journalist and author specialising in travel, art

and gastronomy. She has written about food for several Lonely Planet titles, mostly Southeast Asian and French cuisines, and about cocktails from around the world. You can read more of her work on www.anitaisalska.com.

Virginia Jealous has eaten her way around many countries during almost 20 years of writing for Lonely Planet. When she's home in Denmark (Western Australia, not Europe) she likes to cook her way around places she's yet to visit.

Adam Karlin is a US-based Lonely Planet author who loves to eat, wander and combine the two whenever possible.

Nana Luckham is a one-time editor in London and UN press officer in New York who became a full-time travel writer and has hauled her backpack all over Africa to research guidebooks.

Emily Matchar is a culture writer for magazines and newspapers who has contributed to more than a dozen Lonely Planet titles. Nashville-style chicken would be her jailhouse last meal.

Etain O'Carroll has written and eaten her way across the globe in the name of research over the past 20 years for a host of LP guidebooks, as well as *Food Trails* and *The World's Best Brunches*.

Tom Parker Bowles is an award-winning food

writer and critic who has published five cookbooks, the latest – *Let's Eat Meat* – in 2015 by Pavilion.

Matt Phillips loves his food and has travelled to over 60 countries in search of fine eats, indulging in everything from deep-fried tarantulas and fresh oysters to springbok biltong, all in the name of Lonely Planet research.

Brandon Presser has visited over 110 countries and contributed to more than 50 travel books. He regularly profiles the food world for publications including *The Daily Beast*, *Bloomberg*, and *Travel+Leisure*. He also hosts the American travel TV show, *Tour Group*, on Bravo.

Helen Ranger moved to Fez in 2004, and has been writing about the country ever since, contributing to Lonely Planet's *Fez* and two editions of *Morocco*. Passionate about Moroccan cuisine, she has also contributed to a number of LP books on food and wine.

Sarah Reid is a travel journalist, former Lonely Planet Destination Editor and eternal globetrotter who has sampled the foodie delights of over 70 countries.

Simon Richmond is a writer, photographer and enthusiastic epicurean who has eaten his way around the world enjoying everything from sea urchin in Japan and seaweed lasagne in Cape Town to tapenade on the Côte d'Azur.

Alison Ridgway is a Melbourne-based editor, writer and photographer who has worked at Lonely Planet for 10 years. She has followed her tastebuds across the globe, savouring the strong personal and cultural connections she's made through food experiences.

Daniel Robinson is the author of food reviews – and Lonely Planet guides – to culinary hot spots such as Israel, Tunisia, Cambodia, Borneo, France and Germany.

Phillip Tang has been seduced by anywhere with wafts of charcoal prawns and lemongrass. He writes for Lonely Planet *China*, *Japan*, *Korea*, *Vietnam*, *Mexico*, *Peru* and *Canada*. More photos and food love at philliptang.co.uk.

Luke Waterson writes about the culinary culture of different destinations for publications from Lonely Planet to the *Telegraph*, and on everything from reindeer in Finland to rum in Cuba (www.lukeandhiswords.com).

Penny Watson is based in Hong Kong and writes food and travel articles for newspapers, magazines, guidebooks and coffee-table tomes.

© MYLES NEW / LONELY PLANET

INDEX

BY LOCATION

The World's Best Bowl Food
March 2018
Published by Lonely Planet Global Limited
CRN 554153

www.lonelyplanet.com

2 3 4 5 6 7 8 9 10

Printed in Singapore
ISBN 978 1787 01265 3
© Lonely Planet 2018
© photographers as indicated 2018

Managing Director, Publishing Piers Pickard
Associate Publisher Robin Barton
Commissioning Editor Janine Eberle
Art Director Daniel Di Paolo
Layout Designer Hayley Warnham
Image Researcher Ceri James
Cover Illustration Adam Avery
Editors Lucy Doncaster, Nick Mee
Pre-Press Production Nigel Longuet
Print Production Larissa Frost

Written by Kate Armstrong, Johanna Ashby,
Brett Atkinson, Joe Bindloss, Celeste Brash,
Joshua Samuel Brown, Austin Bush, Lucy Corne,
Janine Eberle, Carolyn B. Heller, Ethan Gelber,
Anita Isalska, Virginia Jealous, Adam Karlin,
Nana Luckham, Emily Matchar, Etain O'Carroll,
Tom Parker Bowles, Matt Phillips, Brandon Presser,
Helen Ranger, Sarah Reid, Simon Richmond,
Alison Ridgway, Daniel Robinson, Phillip Tang,
Luke Waterson, Penny Watson

Lonely Planet Offices

AUSTRALIA
The Malt Store, Level 3, 551 Swanston St,
Carlton, Victoria 3053 T: 03 8379 8000

IRELAND
Digital Depot, Roe Lane (off Thomas St), Digital Hub,
Dublin 8, D08 TCV4

USA
124 Linden St, Oakland, CA 94607 T: 510 250 6400

UK
240 Blackfriars Rd, London SE1 8NW T: 020 3771 5100

STAY IN TOUCH
lonelyplanet.com/contact

Although the authors and Lonely Planet have taken
all reasonable care in preparing this book, we make
no warranty about the accuracy or completeness of
its content and, to the maximum extent permitted,
disclaim all liability from its use.

MIX
Paper from
responsible sources
FSC™ C021741

Paper in this book is certified against the
Forest Stewardship Council™ standards.
FSC™ promotes environmentally responsible,
socially beneficial and economically viable
management of the world's forests.